Arlo Bates

Told in the Gate

Arlo Bates

Told in the Gate

ISBN/EAN: 9783743305052

Manufactured in Europe, USA, Canada, Australia, Japa

Cover: Foto ©ninafisch / pixelio.de

Manufactured and distributed by brebook publishing software (www.brebook.com)

Arlo Bates

Told in the Gate

CONTENTS.

	PAGE
IN THE GATE	7
THE SORROW OF ROHAB	9
THE SWORD OF TAHBER	29
THE CITY OF IREM	47
AHMED	71
THE WIFE OF HASSAN	87
THE RING OF HAROUN AL RASCHID	107
THE VOICE OF SAKINA	169

IN THE GATE.

IN the arched gateway of fair Ispahan,
  Where shadows all day long in ambush lurk
Ready to steal abroad at nightfall, sits
Omar, the story-teller. On his breast,
White as spun-glass, his hoary beard flows down
Until it hides his girdle; his deep eyes
Like cave-set pools in gleaming blackness shine;
His voice is mellow as a drop which falls,
Pure liquid music, in a cistern hewn
From out the living rock. Around him sit
The chief men of the city, they that be
Princes and potentates of Ispahan,
All listening tireless to the tales he tells.

As there they sit at ease, lapped in delight,
Smoking long, fragrant pipes, and nodding grave
Their approbation with high dignity,
The doleful camels burdened pass, the train
Of desert-faring caravan; and veiled
The women walk in unseen loveliness;

While orient lights and perfumes and soft airs
Give to each sweet romance its setting fit;
And each who hears, himself may haply be
Actor in tale as strange as that he lists.

Through the long afternoon like fountain-fall
Runs on the tale till the dim air is sweet
With music of its murmurous syllables,
The liquid, melting cadences which drop
From Omar's lips like honey from the comb.
Spell-bound sit they who hear; while tales like these
Old Omar tells; and long the shadows grow
Of the tall camels passing and of slaves
Who watch their masters, envying their ease
In the cool gateway of fair Ispahan.

THE SORROW OF ROHAB.

THE SORROW OF ROHAB.

I

THE foes of Rohab thrust the tongue in cheek,
　　Smiled in their beards, and muttered each to each;
Fleet messengers went riding north and south
And east and west among the tribes, while bruit
Of discord ever louder waxed, as plots
Begot and hatched in darkness bolder grew,
And showed themselves in day.

　　　　　　　　　　　　As adders held
In a strong grasp writhe to be free and sting,
The hostile tribes had writhed while Rohab's hand
Held them in clutch of steel; but now at last,
When Rohab left the spear to thirst, the sword
To rust undrawn, and heard no sound more harsh
Than the lute's pleading; now that Cintra's love
So filled to overflowing all his heart
That crown and people counted naught, — there rose

A hundred murmurs sinister: the stir
Of foes implacable who knew their time
Had come.

    His people called for Rohab. Fear
Fell like the famine's blight. His nobles came
Up to the doors behind which Rohab dwelt
With joy and Cintra; but the lutes within
Mocked at their suit with merry cadences,
Behind the portals barred. The baser sort,
Angered with fright, and losing fear through fear
More great, sang ribald rhymes about their lord
Under his very lattice; and he heard
Only to smile in hearing. "How a wench,"
They carolled shrilly, "takes the conqueror
To be her plaything! What is Rohab now?
Only an ape that capers to delight
A wanton's leisure!" Stinging ribaldry
The king and Cintra laughed at, though the voice
Of all the land's despair was in the song.

Sedition waxed apace; as rustlings run
Foreboding through the forest when the storm
Gathers its force, through all the army stirred

Murmurs of anger; while the stealthy foe
Crept ever nearer.

     Then, in wrath was half
Despair, by his sire's beard swore Isak, next
To Rohab's self in place and might, that life
And honor though it cost, he would have forth
The king, though he must needs perforce be torn
From Cintra's arms.
      "No living man,"
He muttered, "none, might overcome the king;
But she —"
    And down the dusky corridors
Forbidden to the foot of man he went,
Still muttering in his beard fiercely:
        "But she —!"

II

The smoke of censers, where heaped ambergris
And myrrh and sandal-wood and cinnamon
Fragrantly smouldered, through the languid air
Crept upward, wavering slowly as it rose
To fans of slave girls, whose fair polished limbs
Glowed through the mists of gauzes roseate.
The pearly fall of fountains, and afar
The sound of distant bells, alone broke through
The luscious stillness of the afternoon.

At Cintra's shell-pink feet great Rohab lay,
His mighty body lapped in silken sloth;
While all his soul yearned with love's ecstasies.
One playful finger of her slender hand
Dented his swarthy cheek's rough bronze till white
The pink nail showed, so hard she pressed it in.
Whereat he laughed, and caught the teasing hand,
And kissed it till she laughing drew it back.

Then to escape the burning of his eyes,
She turned and stretched her arm like a swan's neck

After her lute; a shower of pearl, she ran
Her fingers twinkling down the liquid strings,
And broke into a lay, meeting his glance
With eyes where ever love and laughter welled:

"Sweetheart, thy lips are touched with flame;
Sweetheart, thy glowing ardor tame; —
Sweetheart, thy love how can I blame,
    When I, too, feel its fire,
    When all thy fond desire,
Sweetheart, I know the same?

"Sweetheart, thine eyes like rubies glow;
Sweetheart, no more regard me so; —
Sweetheart, I cannot chide thee though,
    Since my looks too are burning,
    Since I, too, throb with yearning;
Sweetheart, thy pangs I know!

"Sweetheart, the blood leaps in thy cheek;
Sweetheart, thy very heart-throbs speak; —
Sweetheart, to chide I am too weak;
    My heart, so hotly beating,
    Is still thy name repeating,
Sweetheart, to still it seek!

"Sweetheart, I touch thy brow;
Sweetheart, I kiss thee now; —
Sweetheart — "

But Rohab dashed the pleading lute aside,
And ended all the lay's soft amorousness
To clasp her in his arms, and kiss her lips
And brow and bosom. Dearer than his fame
Or land or people was his love.
                                 The clang
Of armor and the steps of one in haste
Broke through the monarch's dream. A hand in mail
Tore roughly at the silks of Samarcand
Which veiled the entrance to that nest of bliss.

In one another's arms, but with embrace
Half loosened in amaze that one should dare
Invade that paradise, the lovers looked
With startled eyes as through the portal came
Isak, doom-bearing; and on Cintra's cheek
Instinctive presage turned love's blushes pale.
On Rohab's brow the cloud of mighty wrath
Swelled black as midnight tempest.

THE SORROW OF ROHAB.

"Wherefore this?"
He cried. "Is Rohab counted now so light
His servants seek his face unbidden?"
                                    Word
There was not in reply; but Isak's sword
Hissed in the air, and leaped with burning flash
Downward on Cintra's neck as lightning falls
Upon a lily. Her fair head, with all
Its wealth of hair shining and richly brown
Like melon seeds, its eyes of topaz, lips
Like twin pomegranate blooms, its cheeks as smooth
As a flute's note, all that rare loveliness
Had caught the heart of Rohab as a snare
Tangles the falcon in a coil of death,
Fell, changed to thing of horror, drenched in blood,
And beautiful no more.

                    With cry where rage
Fought mightily with grief, Rohab sprang up,
The rubies on his robe outmatched in red
By blood-drops; while his hand sought for his sword,
But found it not.

                "Thine enemies," in taunt
Cried Isak, "at thy very gates set foot,

And dallying with his love swordless is found
Rohab, the mighty! Slay not me, O King,
Who am a warrior, with a hand perfumed
By playing with thy lady's locks! When thou
Again art Rohab, mine own blade I lend
Till thou avenge this insult on my head.
Now, save thy people!"

       All the dancing girls,
Huddling as sheep crowd when the wolf is come,
Clustered around, but dared not speak or cry.
At Rohab's feet the head that had been she
Lay white and staring-eyed, ghastly. — The king
Set his teeth hard; his eyes were terrible;
Gray his swart cheeks. An instant as clocks count, —
But space how long to their strained souls! — he stood
Immovable.
    "So be it! Go before."

Without one backward glance to where she lay
Whom he had loved, he followed Isak forth.

III

As the simoon which rushes frantic forth
To blast and blight; as the fell swooping wave
An earthquake hurls upon the shuddering shore;
As the dread sword in Azrael's awful hand —
So on his foes fell Rohab. All before
Was pride; behind was shame. Before was strength;
Behind was death. An all-consuming fire
He ravaged; and of twice ten tribes, which bound
Themselves in oath blood-consecrated sword
Nor death itself should stay their bitter way
Till they had conquered Rohab, not one man
Was left to lift the spear. Festered with blood
Was the wide desert, and the vultures, gorged,
Even the scent of carrion could not stir.

His wrath was like the rage of Eblis when
Allah hurled him to hell. The leaping flames
Of thirty cities lighted Cintra's ghost
The darksome way it went. Drunken with blood
And mad with rage, the burning lust to kill
And kill and kill devoured his very soul.

Since she was dead, it stung him to the quick
That any dared be yet alive! He slew
And slew and slew, till there were none to slay;
Till trampled in the blood-drenched dust lay prone
The might of all the tribes.

      Ever the king
Fought with the meanest, with his warriors fared;
And leading once himself a band that stole
To fall upon a village unaware,
While in the thicket crouched, he saw a girl,
Barefooted and barearmed, a peasant maid,
Singing as day went down a song of love,
Twirling her distaff as with shining eyes
She looked across the plain like one who waits:

 "Sings the nightingale to the rose:
  'Without thy love I die!
  Sweetheart, regard my cry!'
 Sings the fountain as it flows:
  'Oh, lily, comfort give;
  Sweetheart, for thee I live!'
 Oh, sweetheart, sweetheart, sweetheart, dear,
 I love thee, and I wait thee here!

"Sings the cyclamen to the bee:
   'In love alone is rest;
    Sweetheart, come to my breast.'
Sings the moon on high to the sea:
   'I shine for thee alone;
    Sweetheart, I am thine own.'
Oh, sweetheart, sweetheart, sweetheart, dear,
I love thee, and I wait thee here!"

And Rohab, cut to heart, drew back his band,
Sparing the village for the sake of her
And for the song whose murmuring burden brought
The memory of another song too sweet,
Too sad to bear.

      Ever at Rohab's side
Where battle's fiercest eddies swirled and raged,
With spume of bloody foam and dreadful wrack
Of broken bodies, trampled man and horse,
Tall spear, proud helm, and vaunting blazoned shield,
All ownerless despite their boast, Isak
Like an avenging angel fought, with sword
That bulwarked Rohab. Thrice he thrust himself
Between the king and blows that would have slain;

Once and again, watching for treachery,
He gave the warning saved the king from foes
Disguised like his own guards and creeping close.
Yet ever Rohab, like one hating life,
Still held his peace, and gave no word of praise.

IV

So wore it till an end was made of war,
And swords were sheathed for very lack of foes.

Prostrate on earth, Rohab, within his tent,
Sorrowed for Cintra, hearing cries of joy
From all the host, and stir of those who shared
The slaves, and noise of those dividing spoil,
And songs of those who revelled, while each cry
Was as a poisoned dart which stung his soul
With festering wound.

    Then came the splendid day
The host gave thanks for victory. The plain
Sparkled with armor like the sunlit sea;
And glowed with colors like a sunset sky.
From every tent-top pennants fluttered gay,
With brave devices wrought in red and gold,
Orange and azure, green and amethyst —
Dragons and monsters, crescents, stars, and all
The arrogant emblaze of heraldry.

Like lithe and glistening water-snakes at play,
That double coil on coil, twist fold on fold,
In brave array the squadrons wound and wheeled,
The air all palpitant with beat of drum
And blare of trumpets, cymbals, horns, and shawms.
Thicker and richer than the butterflies
Above the flower-set meads of Gulistan
A thousand banners waving flew, and plumes
Were as the thistle-down that floats and flies
Where white wild asses feed by Tigris' bank.

So came the army, marching troop by troop,
Where Rohab sat in state to judge his foes
And recompense his heroes.

      After shouts
Which made the banners shake, and joyful noise
Of countless instruments, there came at last
A silence. One by one, war-worn and grim,
Those leaders of the tribes the sword had spared
In bitter mockery of mercy, heard
Their doom of torture with calm front and eyes
Unquailing, prouder in defeat and shame
Than ever in their days of power and pomp.

Then one by one the warriors of the king
Received their mead of richly won rewards
Of gold or glory, with the word of praise
From Rohab's lips, most precious boon of all.
To every troop its tale of spoil was told,
Loot of the tribes in gold and gear and gems.

Last of the host knelt Isak at the throne.

On him with fierce eyes Rohab looked, no word
Loosing his firm-set lips, while Isak drew
His sword from scabbard.
                    "Now, O King," he said,
"That thou again art Rohab, prince of all
Who walk under the stars, I keep my vow.
Take mine own sword and smite."

                          But Rohab stooped,
And raised him to his feet; from his own side
Ungirt the gem-encrusted scabbard.
                              "Nay,"
He answered, "sword for sword. I give thee mine
That all men thus may know whom most the king
Delights to honor."

                        All the circling host
Rent the high heavens with shouting, while the king
With his own hands did on the royal sword
To Isak's thigh.
                    "Rohab the king," he said,
"Honors thy hardihood which did not spare
For fear of death or love of self to slay
His dearest, even in his arms, to save
The land. Rohab the king commends thee; gives
Thee highest grace and praise. Rohab the man —"

He paused for one fierce breath, and all the host
Was still, awed by his wrath; but Isak, pale,
Faced him unflinching, though he read his doom
In the king's blazing eyes.

                            "Rohab the man,"
The bitter words ran on, "cannot forget
How Cintra died. Seek her in Paradise,
Where thou hast sent her; say that her lord's woe
Is as his valor, matchless among men,
And not to be assuaged. Rohab the king
Delights to honor thee. Rohab the man
Avenges Cintra's death, and SMITES!"

                        As fleet
As light the blade that had been Isak's flashed
Downward.   Nor Cintra's blood, nor blood of all
The foes of Rohab it had drunk could glut
Its thirst insatiate as it leaped in greed
To drink its master's.

                        Then when Isak's head
Fell as her lovely head had fallen, death
Were not more silent than the awe-struck host.

But Rohab hid his face, and wept — for her.

THE SWORD OF TAHBER.

THE SWORD OF TAHBER.

I

TAHBER, the swordsmith, chief of all his craft
In fair Damascus, wrought his very soul
Into one splendid weapon. Day and night
Nine months he fashioned it; and said at last:

"This sword instead of my slain son shall be
My wrong's avenger. My heart's blood I give
To temper it. Then, having done my all,
I leave the rest to Allah; He alone
Can sheathe it in the false breast of my foe,
Who sits like Him, enthroned above my reach.
O Allah, righter of all wrongs, receive
This sword, and smite with Thy resistless hand!"

Then over him remembrance of his woe
Swept like a bitter wave that whelms the shore.

"Oh, lost Gulmaar! Oh, my lost son!" he cried;
And, crying, thrust the blade into his heart.

Well all men knew the swordsmith's wrongs. He loved
Beyond all telling his fair wife Gulmaar,
Torment of hearts, world's darling, pearl of love.
To him the halls of Eblis had been heaven
With her; without her, Paradise were hell.
Not all the roses which in glowing bloom
Jewelled Damascus' rose-rich gardens vied
In beauty with her cheeks; no drop which fell
In all its many crystal fountains flashed
With lustre like her eyes; the nightingale
In dim Damascan bowers to its love
Warbled in tones less liquid than her voice.
She swayed the heart of Tahber as the moon
Draws the tide after; and when she had borne
A son fair as herself, and strong of limb
With sturdy promise of his sire's might,
Not Allah's self, throned 'mid His cherubim,
Could thrill with greater rapture than the soul
Of Tahber knew, blest with his wife and child.

But bliss is brittle as an amber bead.
Damascus knew the beauty of Gulmaar;
And as the thistle-down wanders wind-blown,
So rumor of her peerless loveliness
From lip to lip flew lightly till it reached
Even the Caliph's ears in Bagdad. Swift
The Caliph sought Damascus, creeping close,
Like other beast, unto his prey. Who knows
The ways of evil, — and who knows them not?
The Caliph is as Allah in his might;
The Caliph was as Eblis in his lust.
A woman's beauty is the stake she plays
Against the world, and wins her what she may.
Too beautiful for virtue, if Gulmaar
Set her steps to the seeker's, let her veil
Be brushed aside a moment as she passed
Through the bazaar, was it or more or less
Than any woman fair as she and sought
By very Majesty itself, had done?
Who sets his joy upon a woman's faith
Hangs by a cobweb over an abyss.

One night the moon, golden as honey, shone
Upon the swordsmith's garden, and its light

Fell gleaming upon helm and mail and blade
Of them that reft Gulmaar from spouse and child
To glad the Caliph's heart; while her babe lay
Dead by his father's side, who seemed as dead,
So deep the sword-thrusts of the ravishers.

Through the long days in which he struggled back
To life again, as some poor shipwrecked wretch
Fights his way upward through the seething brine,
The bitterest pang which tortured Tahber's soul
Was the accurs'd remembrance that Gulmaar
Chose life in shame rather than death with him.
In burning watches of the night he heard —
Or seemed to hear — the sound of lutes afar;
While visions stung his aching eyes of her,
His pearl, throned in the Caliph's harem. Dead
She still were his, waiting in Paradise;
But living she was lost, and he left lone,
Companionless in the whole universe.

He groped his way to life, and wrought the sword;
Then, in despairing ecstasy of faith,
Set his all on a single throw, and gave
His vengeance into Allah's hand, and died.

II

Throughout Damascus was this story told,
And all men looked on Tahber's sword with fear;
Till from Bokhara came a mighty sheikh,
Who saw the blade and coveted, nor feared
The curse, owning no guilt.   He with him bore
The weapon home; and then Damascus folk
Said to each other:
     "See; the curse has failed.
How can the sword from far Bokhara smite
At Bagdad?"
    Thus they muttered, counting not
That Allah knows not distance nor forgets.

One pearly evening, as in dalliance sweet
The Caliph in his garden with Gulmaar
Reclined beside a fountain, lapped in soft
Warm airs laden with perfumes languorous
Of orange, jasmine, and a thousand blooms,
They heard a wandering minstrel, who passed by
Outside the wall, sing with the voice of fate
A lay which told of that Damascan blade.

The Caliph listened while the song extolled
That marvel of a sword beyond all price
Of gold or jewels, rare as faithful love,
The vanquisher of hosts, — nor yet divined
This steel was cursed for vengeance on his head,
Since none dare vex his ear with Tahber's deed.

"Now by the Prophet's beard, Damascus yields,"
The Caliph jested, "marvels manifold.
Its blades are as its women, matchless. Could
This sword enchant me as thou dost, Gulmaar?"

And still the song ran on, until Gulmaar
In one flash understood, and knew the bard
Told her own tale of shame; yet hiding fear
Beckoned a eunuch as to send reward
Unto the unseen minstrel, singing thus:

> "At Allah's feet he laid his wrongs,
>   In Allah's ear he poured his prayer;
> In his heart's blood baptized his sword,
>   And left the rest to Allah's care.
>
> "The hand of Allah reacheth far,
>   Nor seas nor lands from Him divide:

  In vain earth's utmost bounds they seek
   Who would from Allah's vengeance hide.

"The mind of Allah cannot sleep;
  Alike to Him are rich and poor.
Be it or soon or be it late,
  When Allah strikes vengeance is sure."

The dagger of the eunuch stopped the song,
But terror bit the false heart of Gulmaar.

Then in the Caliph's heart awoke desire
To own that peerless sword; and at his word
Couriers were sent, who brought back word again
How to Bokhara what they sought was gone.
Then vexed that thus his will was crossed, command
The Caliph gave to seek anew the sword,
Nor spare gold in the getting; but Gulmaar
In secret breathed more freely that the curse
For this time was averted; and with wiles
As cunning as a lizard's on the wall
She strove to charm her lord, that he forget
The thing she feared. Glad was she when again
The messengers came back from fruitless quest.

Bokhara's sheikh had sent the fated brand
In tribute unto far-off Astrabad.
                              So seemed
The Caliph's fate to flee him, as full oft
The doom which comes most surely seems to flee
Until the time which Allah doth appoint.
Still teased by the desire which fiercer grew
From being thwarted, yet again he sent
Swift messengers all the long, dangerous way
To Astrabad, as if the whole round world
Stretched its long leagues and deserts wide in vain
To come between the Caliph and his will.

Then in the bosom of Gulmaar arose
A haunting terror, as to one who sees
The shadow of a coming doom steal nigh.
Yet when a third time came with empty hands
The Caliph's messengers, and said: "The sword
We could not buy for gold poured out like sand,
Nor win with pleading;" in her heart leaped up
A triumph insolent, such as false hope
Begets in those whose fall shall bitterest be.
She made this lay, and sang it to her lute,
Soft fluting now, and now shrill-voiced with joy:

"Wine spilled who can gather again?
    Who revive the sweet rose that is dead?
To repine for the past is in vain;
    Never more comes the day that has fled.

"For still what is done, it is done;
    And the word that flies into the air
Cannot alter what fate has begun, —
    For the world is not changed by a prayer.

"A curse is but breath though hearts break;
    And the living need fear not the dead,
Since they sleep far too soundly to wake,
    Since the whole of their story is said!"

So in her triumph lived Gulmaar, with pride
Which like a deadly scarlet fungus sprang.
Each morn more lovely grown, day after day
She wound the Caliph's heart in tighter mesh
Of her enchantments; day by day devised
New revels, fresh delights, and luxuries
Wrung from a starving people, at whose woes
Gulmaar mocked, splendid in her wickedness,
Leading the Caliph on from wrong to wrong,
And matchless in her sins as in her grace; —
While still the sword was far in Astrabad.

III

Trodden beneath the Caliph's feet, like grapes
Crushed in the wine-press till their reeking blood
Splashed all his robes of state, the people lay,
And groaned for mercy, while the heavens seemed brass
Unto their crying. Greed and cruelty
Usurped the place of justice, till the land
Turned like a wounded beast that crouches close
For one last desperate spring, its blood-shot eyes
A-glare with fierceness. Treasons numberless
In secret waxed, like worms which gnaw away
The heart of some great tree burgeoning green
To fall as lightning-smit. The Caliph's son,
Thirsting for power, and poisoned with the taint
Of blood and treachery with which the land
Was festering, devised to steal his crown.
While still the father revelled day by day,
Drinking his fill of wine and love and blood,
And glutted all desires his senses knew,
The son with craft and costly bribes seduced
From his allegiance Bâbec, trusted most
Of them the Caliph still might dare to trust.

Then shameless went the son to fair Gulmaar,
And told her all.
                    "This very night," he said,
"The Caliph falls like a ripe fig, and thou
Wouldst with him fall, but that thy beauty snares
My heart as all men's. Thou shalt reign with me;
And I will give thee seas of bliss for each
Poor drop this peevish dotard doles."
                                        And she,
Too deep of guile to let her heart be read,
Put her slim hand in his and kissed his eyes.

"The Caliph is as dead already," soft
She murmured, "if thy hand against him turn.
I to the living cleave. Sure be thy blow;
Love shall reward thee!"
                          But when he had passed,
Panting and breathless sped she to her lord,
Saying within her heart in bitter scorn:

"Nay, since this Caliph is my slave, I risk
No chance of my dominion. I will win
New favor warning him, and serve myself
In double wise."

                    But as she raised her hand
To part the curtains from the hidden door
Gave entrance to his presence, sharp she paused.
The sound of voices, and the words of one
Who bore the Caliph greeting from afar
Arrested her quick steps; there smote her ear
A word of dread: — one spoke of Astrabad.

Slow is the blooming of fate's aloe-tree;
Swift bursts its flower when the full time is come.
As one who sees a grave yawn at his feet
Where all looked firm ground, stood Gulmaar aghast.
An embassy was come from Astrabad,
Bearing the Sword of Tahber; and one said:

"Commander of the Faithful, not for gold
Our lord would yield this treasure, which he sends
Without price, knowing none on earth save thee,
Who art as Allah, worthy of this steel."

Glad was the Caliph of that gift. He drew
The blade out of its scabbard with a cry,
Gazing in wrapt amazement, while Gulmaar
Peeped shuddering through the curtains, cold with
    fear.

Full glorious was that sword, jewel of war.
Its blade was like a shaft of living light,
Smooth, shining, straight, — yet seeming sinuous
As a snake's tongue while the reflections played
Along its length. Almost it seemed to leap
Out of its haft, so thin it was and slim
Despite its strength. Allah's death angel dread
Smites not with brand more awful or more sharp
Than that embodied terror, edged so keen
It might divide shadow from shadow, cut
Between a rose and its perfume. One side,
In golden letters graved with perfect skill,
"THERE IS NO GOD BUT ALLAH" bore; and one:
"IN ALLAH'S HAND I PUT THIS SWORD, THE CURSE."
Never smith's cunning shaped with flawless art
Marvel more beautiful and terrible.

The Caliph held the sword and turned its blade
Flashing and writhing like a tongue of flame.
He breathed on it to see its brightness cast
The dimness off; and drew his finger-tips
Along its edge with touch like a caress
Laid on the polished bosom of Gulmaar.
Over its beauty fierce he gloated; smiled

With eyes that greedy seemed for blood; nor knew
It was his doom had found him.
                              "Give," he said,
"Dinârs ten thousand to the messenger.
A kingdom's ransom pays a gift like this!"

He turned to Bâbec then, who stood on guard.

"To thee," he said, "I give to wear this sword,
Than which I nothing higher rate save thee.
Such blade in such a hand invincible
Might make a kingdom. Guard my treasure well,
As if it were a tender damsel. See
That it thirst not when there is blood to drink!"

Then Bâbec took the wonder, while Gulmaar
Set her teeth through her lip, so red and full
To call it 'bee-stung' was the Caliph's jest.

"Well shall be done," Bâbec made answer, "all
That is commanded. I will bring the sword
To that end Allah wills."
                          They that stood by,
All save the Caliph only, knew the guile
Was hidden in the word; but he, well pleased,
Fondled his beard, and for the last time smiled

For at that moment from far minaret
The voice of the muezzin fell and called
To prayer the faithful; and Gulmaar, who knew
This was the signal for the Caliph's foes,
Shrieked out in fear, and flung the curtain by.

"Treason!" she cried. "Oh, give not him the sword!"

But Bâbec flashed the blade before her face,
Crying:
      "Nay, it is thirsty, O Gulmaar!
Its time has come to taste again the draught
It drank in Tahber's bosom."
      As he spoke
A tumult rose, and noise of those who came
Rushing with clash of weapons; and Gulmaar,
Faithful at last after life's long unfaith,
Flung her fair body in between the sword
And him it threatened; so that one fierce thrust
Pierced through her breast, which Tahber once had loved,
And sent the blade deep in the Caliph's heart.

Thus Allah with the Sword of Tahber smote.

THE CITY OF IREM.

THE CITY OF IREM.

I

KELÂBAH, wandering through the sun-bleached
    sands
Of Aden, seeking toilsomely the trace
Of his strayed camels, came in very truth
To that lost city, hid from eyes of men,
Sheddâd builded of old ere Allah sent
A sea of wrath to overwhelm his pride.

Mightiest of all earth nourished was Sheddâd,
Like Allah's self in strength and wealth and fame;
But like the sin of Eblis was his sin.
As Eblis, born of fire, refused to bow
To clay-born man, though Allah gave command,
So in his scorn Sheddâd would not bow down
Even to Allah, matching human might
With His who made it.

"All that Allah can,"
Sheddâd had vowed with pride that soared to heaven,
"I can no less. Even that Paradise
Which He hath built on high my hand on earth
Shall far out-build."
     And at his word there rose
Irem, such city as earth had not seen
Till then, nor shall again till Judgment Day.
Far Allah stood aloof till all was done;
But then His lightnings fell, and in a breath
Sheddâd and all his hosts were and were not.
Yet for a sign was Irem left unscorched,
Perfect in beauty; though the eyes of men
Seek it in vain. Invisible it stands
Amid the wastes of Aden till earth fall.

Faithful Kelâbah walked in Allah's sight,
Careful in all the law, and giving alms
To half his substance; but his secret heart
Was cankered with the sin of Eblis, — pride
Like his who builded Irem to his fall.
But Allah, the compassionate, had love
Unto Kelâbah; and in Aden's sands
Led his feet to the gates invisible

Of vanished Irem, showing all things plain,
That he might see the punishment of pride,
And learn how frail is man's best virtuousness.

The camels of Kelâbah strayed away
Into the wastes of Aden, and he went
With one poor camel-driver at his side
Seeking them there; and as they took their way
Kelâbah still dwelt on the law, as one
Who finds his chief delight in holiness.

"Allah," he said, "gives grace beyond account
To those who keep His word; while still His wrath
Falls like the sand-storm upon those who slight
In its least jot the law."
      "Nay; merciful,"
The other answered, "and compassionate
Like mother to her babe, is Allah. Love
Is mightier than the law; nay, love is law."

"Nay," urged Kelâbah, "law is Allah's word,
And Allah's word of all things greatest is.
One pin-prick in the wine-skin spills the wine,
One broken link shatters the chain; and so

Should I in least observance ever fail,
I were accurst as those who worship fire."

"This very morn," the camel-driver said,
"When the muezzin called to sunrise prayer,
I ministered to a sick slave, nor could
I leave his bedside to fulfil the rite.
Yet better pleased I Allah that I stayed
Than had I scores of long prostrations made.
Allah is most compassionate, nor holds
Mercy below the letter of His word.
What Allah is is Allah's highest law."

Then was Kelâbah wroth, and cried:
"Begone!
Herd thou with unbelievers! As for me,
I will no longer walk with one unclean,
Even in this bare waste!"
And all alone
Kelâbah went his way across the sands,
Nursing his virtuous wrath in Allah's name,
And wrapped in sense of his own sanctity.

II

Lone like a lark in level wastes of air,
Or pelican in deserts desolate,
Kelâbah said the sunset prayer, and called
Allah to witness that his faith was firm
Though lost his way and danger all around.
The sands encompassed him about like seas;
The vaulted sky above was thick with stars
As meads at morn with dew-drops. Round and red
The moon rose on his left; and its warm light,
Striking through evening dusks of Aden, gleamed
On domes and towers, and lofty walls of pride,
As if the soft night wind from mist had heaped
A phantom city. Soaring heaven-high
Its towers sprang, their shining whiteness tinged
By the red moon like far peaks sunset-stained.
From roofs of gold the ruddy light was flashed,
While lofty plumes of palm-trees waved between
Like feathery fans above a sultan's head.

Amazed Kelâbah stood, mute with the fear
This vision held some wile of sorcery;

But some power like an unseen hand compelled
His feet on toward the city's gate, which high
Lifted its portals of so awful mien
That man must shrink in awe only to look
Upon their giant front.   Kelâbah bent
As if their simple shadow weighed him down
As he passed through and entered tremblingly
Irem, the beautiful.
     About him rose
The silent city like a dream of night.
Such palaces the dreaming poet sees
Gazing with full heart on the sunset clouds,
Longing to pierce them through, and fill his soul
With sight of Paradise.   Thick stood around
Temples like music rendered visible;
Towers that soared like song; lattice and gate
Like verses sung to a sweet dulcimer
When some fair slave would ravish her lord's ear.
Domes floated light as clouds, with rounded curves
Like a young damsel's bosom ; cornices,
More delicate than lace or shadows cast
By the moon shining through the jasmine vine,
Rimmed the white walls.   On every side there gleamed
Marbles like jewels tinted, precious stones,

Jasper and onyx and chalcedony,
Crystal and alabaster, everywhere
Wrought into cunning shapes of beauteousness,
With mimicry of palm-tree springing tall,
And branch and leaf, and clustered bloom and fruit, ---
So lovely that the hushed heart ached to see.
Gold and enamels gleamed, and arabesques
Which could not but have been — so rich they were —
Stolen from Allah's dwelling.
                            All between,
Fair as love's ecstasies, wide gardens lay,
Where groves of citron grew, thickets of rose,
Myrtle, pomegranate, and the jasmine sweet;
Where fountains sparkling played, and nightingales
Pierced through the moon-lit dusk with shafts of song.

Yet awesome was that city, since no sound
Of human voice or footfall stirred the night.
No faint refrain of distant revellers,
Or noise of busy folk the quiet stirred.
Even that sense of life subtler than air
Which fills a sleeping city with a hum
One rather feels than hears, broke not the calm.
Silent as some lone dwelling of the dead

Where the sad nightingale's heart-piercing lay
Amid the graves makes stillness yet more deep,
Lay Irem, as Kelâbah doubtful passed
From street to street, as one who walks in dreams
Some waste spell-plagued, fearing he knows not what.

Along the moon-white street the echoes mocked
His footfalls' sound with ghostly iterance,
As if pale phantoms followed after. Fear
Struck at Kelâbah's heart, and clutched his throat,
Until he dared not stay, yet feared to flee;
And terror seemed too awful to be borne; —
When sudden to his ear there stole the notes
Of a far lute, which breathed of human cheer
And seemed a call to joy. The warm blood leaped
Once more within his bosom at the sound,
While thrills delicious quickened in his veins.
Such magic was there in that melody
It seemed already to his lips were set
Cups of red wine, while round his neck there stole
The warm arms of fair damsels, formed for love.

Eager his steps he hastened, following on
Whither that luscious strain inviting called.

III

Adown an avenue where on each hand
The tall chinârs, the tree of excellence,
Their splendid plumage waved, Kelâbah went,
Up to a palace portal clustered thick
With carven pillars, painted every hue
The flower-tufted mead can boast in spring.
Onward he pressed through mighty halls, whose tiles
Might shame the choicest jewels in the hoard
Of great King Solomon, into whose hand
The genii gave the richest spoils of earth.
The beams of light from countless silver lamps
As with caressing fingers touched those walls,
And drew their thousand wavering colors forth
As flower-soft girls draw forth bewitching notes
From the clear dulcimer.
      Still, as he went
Ever the lute's enticing fantasies
Sounded more clear, calling his feet to haste
Lest joy elude him which were past all word.
At last he came before a curtain wrought
In silk and gold with matchless imagery;

And put it by, and looked within a room
Where a young damsel lay whose loveliness
Caught his breath from him; till that doorway seemed
Like the lote-tree in Paradise on high,
Beyond which even angels dare not go.

A damsel world-delighting was that maid,
On cushions fair reclining as a leaf
Floats on a fountain's foam. Rich were her robes
Of silk of Yezd, bestrewn with star-thick gems
Brighter than all things earthly save her eyes.
Close to her rosy ear, whose jewel glowed
Like dewdrop on rose-petal, her lute's neck
She pressed, and while Kelâbah stood entranced,
Smitten with love as with a javelin
Flung by a chieftain of the tribes, she sang:

> "The ripe pomegranate bursts,
>   And its crimson juices spill;
> But they cannot stain my mouth, which thirsts
>   To drink of thy kisses its fill,
>   Since my lips are redder still!"

Yet in amaze Kelâbah stood struck dumb,
Wrapt with the song, and dizzy with delight;

While the strain melted into one so soft,
So wooing, and so amorous, that tears
Sprang in his burning eyes, hearing her sing:

  "Oh, sweet is the honeycomb cooled with snow,
      And sweet is thy bosom, warm with love;
  So sweet are remembrances when I must go,
      So sweet when I come is my dove!"

Then playful down the strings her fingers ran,
And mocking in alluring witchery,
She carolled, bending on him night-black eyes,
And laughing till her dimples twinkling shown:

  "The rose leans over the pool;
    Oh, touch me not, touch me not!
  When the sun burns above her,
  The rude bee will love her;
    Oh, touch me not, love!
  When the night breeze is cool —
    Oh, kiss me not, kiss me not!
  With song that pursues her
  The nightingale woos her;
    Oh, touch me not, kiss me not, love!

"The moth to the jasmine flies —
   Oh, touch me not, touch me not!
Drunk with fervid desire,
With love's passionate fire;
   Oh, touch me not, love!
In her bosom he lies,
   Oh, kiss me not, kiss me not!
Till smothered in kisses
He dies of love's blisses;
   Oh, touch me not, kiss me not, love!"

With that she flung the ringing lute aside,
And started from the couch where she reclined,
To take him by the sleeve, and draw him on
Into that chamber decked for love and bliss;
And bow herself before him, murmuring:

"Welcome, O lord and master! I, thy slave,
Have waited long, and wearied for the sound
Of thy feet's coming." White her waving arms
Flashed in the lamp-light as she sprinkled musk,
And seated him on rich brocades of Roum.
Then brought she cakes and fruits, and sweetmeats rare

THE CITY OF IREM. 61

Might make a saint break fast in Ramadhan;
And sherbets cool, and crystal cups of wine;
And handed snowy napkins fringed with gold,
Serving his every wish.
      "Oh, peri-faced,"
Kelâbah cried, "before whose loveliness
The houris must their faces veil in shame,
It is not lawful that I taste thy wine."

With smile constraining more than all the wiles
Of sorcery, she held the cup.
       "Now, nay,"
She said, "within this chamber there is naught
Unlawful save what thwarts my will."
         Her glance
And the sweet fumes of wine mingled to daze
Kelâbah's sense before he tasted. Drunk
With keen delight, scarce knowing what he did,
He who had never failed in all the law,
Took up the cup; and she, seeing it turn
From ruby into crystal as he drank,
Clapped her small hands till all her bangles rang,
And laughed in glee.
     "Now thou art mine indeed,"
She cried, "as I am thine. O lord and love,

How long and long and long have been the days
Since foot of man along these silent streets
Awoke the echoes querulous to complain.
Love, by my faithful waiting for this hour,
Am I not thine?"
      And seething in his blood
Kelâbah felt the fires of wine and love.

"Yea, thou art mine," he answered. "I am thine.
Kiss me, and clasp me close, and let thine heart
Beat on my breast, thou moon of love!"
        But she
Drew back a little, and with beckoning hand
Called him to follow after as she led
Through rooms where amber-perfumed lamps lit up
Such splendors as the heart of love-mad king,
Straining to image dwelling worthy her
Whom he adores, could never dream.
        At last
A door of aloe-wood with silver bound,
Inlaid with ivory and pearl, and set
With turquoise and with coral, barred their way.
The damsel pushed it back until he saw
A shrine with jewels crusted like a cave;

Where, on an altar wrought of beaten brass,
There burned a flame, fed with all precious woods
And ambergris and spice and frankincense.
Then bending her slim neck as in the wind
The snowy poppy bends, the damsel bowed
In reverence at that shrine.
      Kelâbah saw
With thrill of horror.
      "Out, accursed one,"
He cried, "who bows to fire! Can this thin flame
Prevent that now I slay thee?"
        But she turned
And looked on him with eyes before whose glow
His holy zeal melted as smoke in air.

"Nay, bear with me, belovéd," soft she said.
"Since all this place is held beneath a spell.
It is to save thy life that I salute
This flame; and thou, wouldst thou but join with me
In adoration, might deliver me,
And lead me forth from Irem the accurséd
To be thine own forever!"
       But he cried,
With kindling cheek and eyes ablaze with wrath:

"*I* bow down at this altar ! *I* revere
The flame profane ! Allah shall smite thy mouth
If thou again — "
                                      But that fair damsel laid
Her down-soft fingers on his lip, and hushed
The word he would have said.
                                        "'T is as thou wilt,"
She murmured, " though it be that my heart break !
Save me or leave me, for thou art my lord,
And I am but thine handmaid."
                                            Limpid tears
Swam in her night-black eyes, while bending sad
She like a broken tulip drooped ; till he
Could not but clasp her in his eager arms,
Kissing and comforting. Then tempting him
She swayed her rest-destroying body, fair
As a rose-tinted pearl, and let her locks,
Black as the gloom in wastes beyond Mount Kaf,
Fall on his hands, a perfumed cataract ;
And sighed, and broke her sighs with choking
    sobs ;
And bathed her face in waters of deceit,
Beguiling him, and won him till no will
He had which was not hers, but yielded all.

"O cypress, musk-perfumed," he cried at last;
"To save thee from this spell there is no deed
Which can be evil. If in truth I sin,
Allah, who made thee, knows that Paradise
Were not too dear a price to buy thy love."

Then prone before that leaping flame he fell
Adoring, while the damsel near him bowed,
Hiding her wicked laughter from his eyes.

Then springing to her feet, the damsel took
Kelâbah by his hand, and laughing led
Adown more corridors, across new halls,
And through fresh gardens. Never word was born
In which their beauty might be told; on earth
No thing to which they might be likened, since
Irem was never matched in loveliness.
And seeing only her whose warm hand thrilled
His every nerve, Kelâbah followed on,
While down the moon-washed street she hurried him,
And brought him to the city's gate at last.

"Thou hast delivered me," she said, her voice
Softer than plash of wave on level sands.

"Since great Sheddâd was smitten has my doom
Held me enchained amid this solitude
Till one who worshipped Allah should be snared
By my allurements to adore the flame.
Thou hast delivered me, and I am thine.
Oh, my belovéd, look upon me now
In my true shape; see if I be not fair!"

Speaking, she drew him outward through the gate
Into the wastes of Aden. Ere his heart
Could give one throb, in the abyss of night
Irem had vanished, and as tender rose
Thrust in a torch's flame shrivels and blights,
So that fair damsel, even with his arm
Clasped round her, changed to sudden hideousness.
Ghastly and old, throated like pelican,
With gaunt, thin bosom, and gray, weed-like hair,
Was she who, grinning, to Kelâbah clung;
As horrible as a foul ghoul which plucks
Pale corpses limb from limb among the graves
In feasts unholy. Like a wretch who lays
His hand upon a leper unawares,
Kelâbah shrieked, and would have fled, while she,

Frighting the wandering jackals of the waste
With laughter harsher than their own, cried out:

"Am I not thine, Kelâbah? Hast thou not
To win my beauty bartered Paradise?
Kiss me, and take thy joy of my sweet mouth!"

But mad with loathing and with fear he fled,
Caring not whither, till at last he fell
Headlong upon the sand, and knew no more.

IV

Dreams horrible as vaporous shapes from hell
Crowded Kelâbah's sleep, until he felt
A touch upon his shoulder, and awoke.

Long level beams, like bars of beaten gold,
The rising sun stretched far across the waste;
Bathed in its glow the camel-driver bent
To lift him up.
    "Awake; arise," he said.
"All the long night I sought thee through the waste,
Fearing some evil had befallen thee.
Arise, and make profession of thy faith;
Already ends the hour of morning prayer."

But prone Kelâbah lay, and hid his face,
Groaning in shame and anguish.
     "Nay," he moaned,
"Would I had never waked, for I have sinned
Beyond all pardon, and adored the flame.
Leave me to perish in the wilderness,
Who am unclean, lest Allah smite thee down
If thou consortest with the infidel."

But at his side the camel-driver knelt,
And lifted him, and said :
                              " Be yet of cheer ;
For merciful and most compassionate
Is Allah. Be thou sure the hand that made
Knoweth the weakness of its handiwork ;
Pities man's frailty and forgives his sin.
There is no god but Allah ; in His name
I bid thee rise and pray."
                         And in the waste
Kelâbah bowed his head, while all his pride
Fell from him swift as fled the loveliness
Of that alluring fiend who tempted him.
And thenceforth, evermore remembering
Irem, in Allah's sight humble he walked,
Till all his life in tender beauty shone
With meekness like the lustre of a pearl.

AHMED.

AHMED.

I

AHMED, the slave, painter of tiles, was blessed
    By Allah with a skill so rare and fine
That hardly nature with more cunning laid
Her thousand tints on leaf and flower. His brush
With such deft mimicry portrayed a rose
As to deceive the amorous nightingale;
Under his hand grew such sweet witchery
Of bud and bloom, and arabesque, and scroll
With text of holy Koran writ thereon,
That all men wondered; so that near and far
His work was sought, and that mosque counted rich
Whose walls his handiwork adorned. Across
His tiles the swift birds darted, bright of hue
And full of life as in the skies; though each
Bore on its neck the fatal line which marked
It dead; since "Image of no living thing,"

The Prophet hath commanded, "shalt thou make,
Lest Allah on the Last Day at thy hand
Demand a life to animate this form
Of life which thou hast wrought."

                                                  In his rude hut
Content dwelt Ahmed in humility,
And day by day wrought at his art, nor longed
For aught beyond, happy amid his tiles.
But man's life changes as the rainbow hues
Upon the preening peacock's plumage change;
And man's heart is as dust upon the wind,
Swept here and there as passion's gusts may blow.
Happy lived Ahmed, though he was a slave,
Until that day the Cadi's daughter passed,
The damsel Elka, with her eyes of light,
Kindlers of storm, the torches of desire;
Then all his peace and calm melted away
As shadows in a sudden sun-burst fade.
It was but one swift glimpse behind her veil,
Brief as a sigh, yet all eternity
By that quick glance was altered. Elka passed,
And went by all unheeding, unaware
Ahmed had seen her passion-kindling face,

That all his soul waxed fervent as with flame.
To her the slave who painted at his tiles,
Though his brush cunning were as nature's own,
Was as the grass between the pavement stones,
The tuft of basil nodding on the wall,
Or any trivial, unregarded thing.

But Ahmed was no more a slave. His soul
Sprang up new-born, as one whom Allah calls
Out of a clod to being. Now for him
The nightingale sang in the thicket; now
For him the rose with perfume drenched the air;
Now first for him the sun rose in the morn;
And now for him the stars glowed in the skies,
Bringing the message of eternity.
His soul was quickened till he understood
How all things are of love, how love is all.
The day was eloquent with thoughts of her,
The night rich with the rapture of its dreams.
The heaped-up jewels of the dim bazaar,
The splendors of the morn, the thrills of night,
The bright hues dabbled by his cunning brush,
Warmed him with sweet remembrances, which seemed
Part of her life since they were beautiful.

If a chance word of love fell on his ear
He seemed to hear her name, and see again
Her face behind its veil.   The call to prayer
Seemed but a cry from the tall minaret
That all men do her homage.   If one sang,
The heart of Ahmed leaped to join the lay
And pour its longing forth.

       One song there was
He heard the slave girls sing, which evermore
Seethed in his blood like potent Shiraz wine:

  The rose as it lies on thy bosom
   Is cradled as light as in air;
  The cloud of the midnight tempest
   Is not so black as thine hair;
  The red of thy cheek's surrender,
   When love overcometh pride,
  Is like the brown dusk's splendor
   Where sunset hues have died.

  At sound of thy voice, in the thicket
   The nightingale hideth shamed;
  Beside the arch of thine eyebrow
   The crescent moon is blamed.

As smoke toward heaven ascending
   Through the still and perfumed air,
In grace all perfect bending
   Swayeth thy body fair.

Yet Allah into His heaven
   Can never let thee come,
Lest sight of thy loveliness surely
   Should strike His angels dumb.
But not for that I forsake thee;
   I will follow to nethermost hell,
Till Allah for envy shall hate me,
   Because of thy beauty's spell!

II

Then in his passion and his loneliness,
Mad with the sweet and cruel smart of love,
In secret Ahmed sinned. With eager brush,
And all the skill of heart and brain on fire,
He painted on a slab of ivory
Elka's fair semblance; there he imaged forth
Her cheeks flushed like an apricot; the brow
Which from her night of hair gleamed like the moon;
The eyes like stars reflected in a pool;
Lips like the rainbow arched; the tender breasts
Curved like a shoreward wave and white as snows
On sky-touched Caucasus. But when her neck
A tower of silver, grew beneath his brush,
His heart forbade him, and he crossed it not
With that faint line of death to signify
That this was image of no living thing.
The Judgment Day was far and love was near.

So one by one the days were born and died
Like angels born of fire who chant one song
In Allah's praise and as a mist-wreath fade.

Still Ahmed painted at his tiles and dreamed,
Loving a shadow; till there came an hour
He clasped her in his arms and spoke her name.

It chanced a crowd of camel-drivers thronged
Hurrying along the street where Ahmed dwelt,
Glad that the end was come of the long march
Across the desert in the caravan;
And as their beasts, laden with precious bales
Of silks of Samarcand and gems from far,
Amber and coral, sandal-oil and spice,
Turquoise and ambergris and beaten gold,
Jostled each other in the narrow way,
The Cadi's daughter and her slave girl passed.
Painting in characters of sapphire blue
The Koran's words which praise the Prophet's bride
Sat Ahmed, when he heard a cry. Some sense
More keen than reason made him spring to save
The damsel whom he loved, pressed to the wall
By the rude travellers. A moment brief
As a bell's note but sweet as Paradise,
He clasped her close, and drew her to his hut
Till the tall camels passed. He felt her heart
Beat like a netted dove; but when she drew

Bright sequins from her girdle, he put by
The gold she proffered, kissing her robe's hem,
While all his being melted with desire.
With flame so fierce his passion waxed, it seemed
He had not loved till then. He spoke her name,
Which blessed his lips as the wild honey-comb,
Dripping from crevice of a lonely rock,
Refreshes the starved wayfarer.
       That night
Around the Cadi's garden, to and fro,
He wandered like a restless djinn accursed
Outside the walls of Paradise. Within
He heard an amorous lute complain, while soft
A nightingale broke in upon each pause
Till all the dusky night seemed full of love;
And almost Ahmed swooned, remembering not
That he was but a slave who painted tiles.

But on the morrow came a word which fell
Like an envenomed dart on Ahmed's soul.
The slave of Elka, hurrying on her way
To the bazaar, lingered to whisper:
         "Lo,
I know thou lovest her, but her slim hands

Are henna-stained for marriage.   Love her not,
And I — am I not fair? — will comfort thee."

But Ahmed stood amazed, like one struck dumb
A breathing space, and then with bitter word
Burst forth in rage:
     "Thy breast be spit upon,
Foul witch, for this thy lie!   Beyond Mount Kaf
Thy bones be strewn, and Eblis have thy soul!
Thou broken potsherd, callest thyself fair,
When she, a vase of crystal without flaw,
Is named?"
    The slave girl fled in fear, and cried:

"This potter curses like a Caliph!   Lo,
Who apes the loves of princes apes their wrath.
Allah be merciful, but he is mad!"

III

Long hours Ahmed brooded in his hut
Over her picture; till the sun of noon
Made all the thin leaves of the tamarisk
Droop with the fervent heat. Then with a cry
Of one whose reason flees, he rent his clothes,
And ran half naked through the burning streets
To Elka's dwelling. Guardless were the doors,
And Ahmed sped into the palace, mad
With love and fury.

     All about the court
He found them that made ready for the feast,
And everywhere the signs of coming joys;
Slaves hasting to and fro with stuffs and robes,
And busy merchants coming with their wares,
Confectioners and caterers in throngs.

As a fierce leopard falls on peaceful flocks
In Rocnabad, fell Ahmed on the slaves,
And flung upon the ground their dainty cates.
He trampled in the dust the glowing heaps

Of grapes and melons, plums and apricots,
And heaped pomegranates; broke the crystal bowls
Brimming with topaz syrups; dashed to earth
The jars of mountain snow which should have cooled
The bridal sherbets. Shrieks of rage and fear
Arose in tumult. All the eunuchs fled
Before his fury, while his bitter wrath
Blazed ever fiercer till it spent itself
As a spent flame for want of fuel dies.
And some cried: " Lo, a fiend is in him!" Some:
" Allah with madness smites him!" But all fled.

He turned and ran on blindly, knowing not
Whither he went, until he was alone
In a dim chamber where the slave girls peered,
Huddling with dread outside the curtained door.
Then, for that love and madness move to tears,
He flung himself on earth and called her name,
And wept upon her picture, as one weeps
On the belovéd's bosom.

                     Then in haste
There came to Elka her own slave, who loved
Ahmed in very truth.

                        " Breaker of hearts,"
She said, "Ahmed, the cunning painter, he
Who saved thee from the camels' feet, and whom
Allah hath made most beauteous among men,
And dowered with skill that all men wonder at,
Is mad for love of thee, and through the court,
Ravages like a wolf, till all are fled
In fear before his face."

                        To that dim room
Where Ahmed crouched, a miracle of woe,
Prating wild words, and with fierce, fevered eyes
Gloating upon her image painted fair,
Came Elka, all unveiled, with ankle-bells
That tinkled as she walked, her beauty rich
Like the full moon in its persuasiveness,
Her eyes like very stars. She touched his brow
With her slim fingers, henna-stained, and looked
Into his restless eyes, compassionate,
As one who knew and pitied all his woe.
And twice her sweet lips parted, ere her voice
She could command to speak.
                            "Alas!" she said,
"There is no god but Allah; in His name

Be peace to Ahmed.   In the Judgment Day
When Allah bids thee to mine image here,
Which thou hast made, give life and breath at last,
How wilt thou answer, Ahmed?"

                                    Straight there fell
A silence in his whirling brain, a calm
Which seemed to pierce his madness through as strikes
The sun through mists.   He grovelled in the dust,
Embracing her small feet, whose instep's arch
Sprang like the city gate.

                          "In Allah's name
Be peace to thee," he said, "and bridal joy
Beyond all measure.   Surely I have sinned;
And rashly raised a slave's eyes to thy face.
But, for this image of thy loveliness,
I give my own life that it lack not breath
In that great Day of Resurrection ; yield
My very soul to be its spirit."

                                        Thus
He spoke, his madness gone, and looked on her
As one looks back on a lost Paradise;

Then left her there alone, bathed in her tears.
And no man looked on Ahmed more, or knew
How he invoked the sword of Azrael.

But when at the Last Day Allah shall call
All beings that have life before His bar,
There will two Elkas be, but in all space
Nowhere Ahmed, the slave, painter of tiles.

THE WIFE OF HASSAN.

THE WIFE OF HASSAN.

I

DEAR to the Caliph was the gift of song.
　　Of all the joys which minister delight
There was none, save love only, which he prized
Above the poet's art.　More than in gold
Or in the hoarded jewels heaped to burn
Like smouldering fires in his treasure-house,
He joyed in precious verse; and welcome still
Minstrel and poet ever were to him
As to the caravan the desert well.
Who could command his art with cunning skill
And melt beguiling measures into song,
Might ask the Caliph whatsoe'er he would
And win a rich reward.　Justice might fail,
And wrongs be cried in vain before his throne;
But when the poet's soft persuasiveness
Besieged the Caliph's ear, it could not fail
To win its suit.

It chanced one summer day
When stretched amid his silken cushions, prone
In sloth luxurious the Caliph yawned,
Wearied of dancing-girls, and vexed at heart
With the insatiable, dull weariness
Of full satiety, there came a slave
With word of an Arabian, who would fain
Caress the Caliph's ear with story wrought
Into a poem.

"By the Prophet's beard,"
The Caliph said, "in good time is he come.
Let him be brought, and if his skill avail
To kill the tedium of this weary hour,
His weight in gold dinârs shall pay his song."

So was the young Arabian ushered in;
Straight as a date-palm of the wilderness,
Lithe as a leopard, sinewy as a wolf,
With eyes like drops of myrrh which liquid gush,
Goldenly brown, from the bruised tree, he stood
Before the Caliph, his prostrations made,
Waiting command to speak.

"Whence dost thou come?"
The Caliph questioned; "and how art thou called?"

"Commander of the Faithful," said the youth,
"In Cufa, where I dwell, thy servant's name
Is Hassan called. Will my most gracious lord
Have patience with his slave while I recite
This poem I have made, as one might weave
A basket out of rushes that it serve
To béar sweet blossoms unto her he loves? —
Since so these verses bear my reverence
Unto my gracious lord."

                        "Say on," with smile
The Caliph answered. "As thy mistress' self
Smelling the fragrance of thy flowers rush-bound
In all complaisance will we hear."

                                A light
Flashed up in Hassan's eyes, the look of one
Who stakes his all in hope, and sees the prize
Already in his grasp. He waited not
For further word, but with firm, winning voice,
Softened to music in the rhythmic verse,
Began his tale. As waters gurgling flow
Poured from a vase of alabaster, clear
The liquid, interlacing syllables
Of that lay fell, sense married unto sound

As threads of silk intwine with strands of gold
When cunning workmen weave brocades of Roum.

And the lay told how in a lovely vale,
Set 'round with wild chinâr-trees, lined with turf
As a lark's nest with down, and gemmed with flowers
Thick as the sparkles on the sea, there dwelt
A maid tender and fair as a babe's eyes,
Pure as a dewdrop in a lupin leaf,
And sweeter than the songs of Paradise.
As the moon brings the dew, so she brought love
Unto all hearts, and where Zuleika came
Her beauty and her goodness lustre shed
As spring wakes buds to bloom, and gentle rain
Brings life to the parched earth, weary with drought.
All men desired her, but her true heart
Was given to a shepherd, who with song
Had wooed her in the long, sweet afternoons,
And dusky eves when fire-flies, as thick
As golden motes which dance in the long beams
Of sunset, flashed amid the camphor-trees.

Then of their love the poet told, while tears
Swam in his eyes, as he himself had known

The ecstasy of her affection.   One
In heart and soul were they, bound in fond ties
Even before her fingers, henna-stained,
Were clasped by him her spouse.   The poet's voice
Dropped low, like that of one remembering
Some precious past, as he recalled a song
The shepherd sang his love forbidding doubt:

"Oh, can night doubt its star, the dawn its sun?
Can rivers doubt the sea to which they run?
No more canst thou doubt me, heart's dearest one!
   Doubt is the darkness, love the light;
     Doubt is the night, and love the day;
     Doubt is this earth which takes its flight;
       But love is Heaven that lasts alway!"

And the tale told how in that vale they lived,
Joying in one another, till ill chance
Brought thither Cufa's governor; and how
He strove to win Zuleika's love with arts
Of wicked guile; and tempted her true heart
With proffered gifts, and dazzling promises,
But could not touch her faith or shake her love.

And how he fell upon that peaceful vale
As falls a falcon fierce upon a nest
Of half-fledged, helpless nightingales, and bore
Zuleika, ravished from her husband's arms,
To be a gem for his own wearing.
                                        Soft
With tender words the poet told the woe
Of that sad shepherd who was thus bereft;
Then turning his smooth verse with cunning art
Into a strain which like war's clarions rang,
He breathed the panting rage came next; the mad,
Wild passion to avenge that bitter wrong.
Then with long plaintive syllables, the lay,
In cadences which fell like scalding tears,
Painted the awful blackness of despair
Which came upon the shepherd, seeing might
Triumphant raised above his weakness' reach.

The Caliph felt his own eyes over-brim;
Forgot his snow-cooled sherbet, pink with juice
Of sweet pomegranates, as he eager leaned
More close to catch the poet's every word;
And hung upon the lay as if the tale
Voiced his own woe.

                    Then as a lute-player
Hushes his strings' complaint lest all too keen
The anguish of the strain, the poet changed,
And told how on that night of sorrow rose
A star of hope.   There came a messenger
From lost Zuleika, saying: "Faithful still,
I yet am thine, and scorn the Cadi's love.
Fly to the Caliph ; help is his alone.
Beseech him that he right this heinous wrong,
And save and give me to thine arms again!"
Then, knowing that the Caliph is as God,
Gracious and strong and most compassionate,
That lover-spouse bereft, with eager feet
Unto the Caliph hasted, in his ear
Pouring the story of his grief, with cry
For help and succor in his piteous need.

The poet ceased, and so full silence fell
They heard the doves, in the still afternoon,
Croon in the court without.   The Caliph sat
Upright among the silken cushions strewn
On the divan unheeded.

                        "What is next?"
He cried.   "What said the Caliph?"

                        At his feet
The poet knelt.
                "The rest is as thou wilt,
And as thou doest," was his pleading cry.
"O lord of all men, this is mine own wrong;
And no help have I if thou wilt not hear.
A captive in the Cadi's hand is she
Who is my wife and love; who is my all.
Save her and me, in Allah's gracious name!"

"Now by the Prophet's beard!" the Caliph cried;
"Thy lay hath won this boon. This very hour
Shall messengers depart for Cufa, swift
To bring again thy wife."

                        And at his word
Hassan fell prone, swooning for very joy.

II

Ill brooks the Caliph that which thwarts his will;
And wroth was he when back his couriers came,
Saying:
   "Commander of the Faithful, lo,
The Cadi is enamoured of his prize
Even to madness. All he hath and is,
His wealth and life alike, he gives to buy
Her dear companionship for six short moons,
Although she loves him not."

       "Now by mine eyes!"
The Caliph cried in furious anger, "sure
This rebel sends me not such answer twice.
Bring me this woman and the Cadi's head."

But when they went to do his will, he looked
On Hassan musing, murmuring in his beard:

"What is this woman that six moons with her,
Even without her love, is worth a life?
Perchance the praises which this poet sung

Were not all empty words, strung down his lay
Like pearls in a maid's hair."
                              And vexed was he
At every lagging moment till she came;
While Hassan joyed that vengeance thus should fall
On him who tore Zuleika from his arms,
And glowed with bliss that she should come again.

The night swallowed the day, and bounteously
Allah a new day gave, and gave again;
And with the third day came the messengers,
Bearing a ghastly head stained black with blood,
And Hassan's wife, for whose sweet sake the sword
Had shorn it from the Cadi.
                              Tall was she,
Fair as Zohara, who at Babel snared
The angels to their fall.   In her lone vale
Had waxed her beauty till it smote like fate,
As the chinâr-tree springs to majesty
Even in arid wastes.   She came unveiled,
As Arab women use, and her dark eyes
Like clash of cymbals woke the Caliph's heart.
But when she spoke, her voice so exquisite,
Shaming the lute to modes of sadness tuned,

Melted the heart more than her loveliness;
While yet the wisdom of her witching tongue,
Her playful sorcery of wit, surpassed
The melody of her sweet voice.
                            No more
The black-eyed damsels, moons of love,
Who ministered to his delight, and bent
As graceful in the dance as rushes bend
When wakes the night wind, to the Caliph seemed
Fair among women. Her melodious voice
Made harsh their singing; while their babbled words
Were as the dry cicada's teasing note
After her eloquence. Love's fever burned
In all his veins, till even Paradise
With all its houris tempted him no more.

Three days he fought his passion, keeping her
Apart from Hassan; then he could no more;
But spoke hot words of love, and bade her cast
Her shepherd spouse aside, to reign with him.

"My power and state," he vowed, "all that I have
Shall be thine own no less than it is mine.
Thou hast ensnared my heart; I have and am

Nothing which is not thine. Thine eyes for me
Are like the wells of Paradise; thy voice
Sweeter than flute-note or the dulcimer
Whose strings are smit by amorous Indian maid;
Thy bosom's swell tears my heart from me; sighs
Of longing love consume my panting breath
When thou art nigh!"

                                            But fair Zuleika raised
Her glance to his, and catching up a lute
Which lay on the divan, sang to him thus:

> "The rose on love's bosom may lie,
>   But who would the pimpernel wear?
> The pearl with the ruby may vie,
>   But who for the dewdrop doth care?
> I am naught but the dewdrop which flows,
>   I am naught but the pimpernel mean;
> Take thy joy of the pearl and the rose;
>   Let the pimpernel wither unseen."

But he broke in upon her song, and cried:

"Nay; but the sun seeks out the pimpernel,
And drinks the dew; as I must make thee mine!

Hear me, Zuleika; shall thy beauty be
Hid in the desert? All thy dainty wit
Be spent on senseless ears; thy days go by
In tedious weaving goat's hair for the tents,
In making cheeses out of camel's milk,
And all the petty toils of slave girls rude?
Leave these things for a kingdom; help me rule;
And I will be thy slave no less than lord."

But she drew back, and bent, and answered him:

"Commander of the Faithful, mock me not,
Making in jest a trial of my faith."

"Nay, by the Prophet's beard," the Caliph swore,
"I jest not. Think what I can offer thee,
And cleave not to this shepherd. All the joys
Of Paradise shall on this earth be thine."

"And after earth," she said, "shall still the joys
Of Paradise be mine? Do not this sin
Lest Allah smite thee!"
                        Then with sudden tears,
She fell down at the Caliph's feet, and cried:

"Have mercy, O thou lord of life, and spare;
For thy handmaiden loveth him! For me
There is no man on earth save Hassan. Life
Is life no longer if I be not his.
His heart and mine are one. His faith in me
Is as his trust in Allah."

      "Now, then, nay;"
The Caliph scoffed; "for never was man's faith
In woman like her faith in man. Prove him;
And if he doubt thee not on my bare word
I yield thee to him."

      Up Zuleika sprang,
Splendid in pride and trust; and raised her hand
As a lark flies to heaven.

      "Now if he doubt
For one brief heart-beat; if indeed so much
As his glance falter, I will be thy slave
Till Asrael smite me."

      So the proof to make
The Caliph summoned Hassan, sore at heart
Because Zuleika was kept from him.

                              " Thou,"
The Caliph said, "who lov'st Zuleika well,
And need'st must wish her well, canst but rejoice
That she henceforth is queen, to share with me
My wealth and throne. She sends thee her farewell;
And bids thee ask what precious boon thou wilt,
Slave girls or gold or camels, to take back
As proof of her remembrance to thy vale."

But Hassan stood erect with folded arms,
And looked into the Caliph's face unmoved.

"It is a lie," he said. "Thou couldst constrain
Zuleika's body, but her heart is mine,
Changeless and faithful till the Judgment Day."

And from behind the curtain where she hid,
Zuleika burst in haste, and flung herself
At Hassan's feet, kissing them while for joy
She wept and laughed at once. She raised her hands
To heaven and to the Caliph, crying still:

"Allah is witness that he did not doubt!"

The dark blood stained the Caliph's cheek, while rage
Flashed in his eyes as when the lightning plays
Around the icy cone of Demavend.

"I still am Caliph," in his heart he said.
"What hinders me from having Hassan slain,
That so Zuleika, spite of all, be mine?"

But she, guessing the thought was in his mind,
Turned upon him her star-bright eyes, and said:

"Yet Allah knoweth had he doubted, death
Had been Zuleika's refuge; not the arms
Of any other man upon the earth."

An instant their two glances met like those
Of two fierce falcons. Then he turned aside
As if he dared not look on her again.
"Go!" was his only word.

                              And they went forth,
Back to the solitude of that fair vale,
Wrapt in the sweet contentment of their love.

Then after them the lonely Caliph sent
A tall white camel, laden with rich bales

Of precious stuffs, that beauty such as hers
Lack not fit setting; but in Hassan's eyes
Zuleika's loveliness had little need
Of stuffs or pearls; her faithfulness and love
To him were gems of worth surpassing far
The richest jewels in the Caliph's store.

THE RING OF HAROUN AL RASCHID.

THE RING OF HAROUN AL RASCHID.

I

AL MOHDI, father of the great Haroun,
  Lay dying in his tent at Masabdan;
And longed and prayed amid his burning pangs,
That he might see his son before he died.

Best of his sons Al Mohdi loved Haroun;
And schemed how he might give to him the throne
Which right gave to Al Hadi, elder born.
Three times he had sent trusty messengers
Unto Haroun, praying him come with speed,
That they might plot together; but Haroun
Would not.
            " Al Hadi's is the throne," he said.
" Allah, who sent him first into the world,
Gave him to wear the crown, and me has made
His subject and his brother.   Not for me

A stolen throne, where one shall shameless sit,
Tainted with reek of a slain brother's blood,
A living lie in Allah's sight and man's."

Then was Al Mohdi grieved to very heart,
Nor could he rest; but he must needs set forth,
Hastening to find Haroun, and wake in him
Ambition's greedy avarice of power.
But there in Masabdan lay treacherous death
In ambush in his way, and smote him down.

Two damsels, moons of love, the Caliph took
To cheer his journey. Both the slaves were fair,
Provoking love, beguiling amorous eyes,
And both were dear unto Al Mohdi's heart;
But better loved he Fâtima, a girl
Whose dark eyes first had blessed the light of day
In a fair valley of Cashmere. Her lips
Had caught the music of the waterfall
Whose tinkling murmur lulled her cradled sleep,
A rose-lipped baby in her father's hut;
And to the Caliph her melodious voice
Was sweeter than the fluting of soft pipes
That all his soul subdued to her dear will.

But Hâsana, her fellow-slave, at heart
Hated fair Fâtima with jealousy
Remorseless as a flame, yet cunning hid
Her hate under affection's guise, and praised
The Caliph's choice when he heaped priceless gifts
On her he loved; while still her bitter heart
Lay like an ambushed snake, waiting the time
When it might spring and strike. Thus it befell
That there in Masabdan she smiling gave
To Fâtima a poisoned apricot,
So fair, so fragrant, and so melting ripe
That hardly could the eager mouth refrain
From tasting its seductive juiciness.
But Fâtima into the Caliph's hand
Yielded the gift, that here in Masabdan
Its fragrance and its savor bring to mind
His gardens in far Bagdad; and she sat
Beside him singing lightly while he ate
The luscious, spicy sweetness of the fruit:

> "Love's like a summer rose
>   Whose fragrant buds unclose;
> But ah, how soon it goes,
>   Fading and wasting!

Fallen its petals lie,
Quickly to fade and die, —
Thus do love's pleasures fly,
    Lost in the tasting.

"Yet as new roses blow,
As fresher fountains flow,
So will new raptures glow,
    New joys delight thee;
Lips that entreating press,
Arms warm in soft caress,
Bosoms of loveliness,
    To bliss invite thee.

"Is not the new love fair?
Why for the old despair?
As song dies on the air
    So love is fleeting.
Why then the past regret?
Pleasure remaineth yet;
Love only and forget
    Memory's entreating!"

And even as she sang the dart of death
Struck down the Caliph, taken in the snare
False Hâsana had spread for Fâtima.

Three days and nights Al Mohdi fought with death,
While couriers fleet-footed sped like men
In terror of their lives to bring Haroun.

Swift as a meteor which flashes down
Brief past the steadfast stars, onward Haroun
Rode through chill, shivering night, through burning day.
His Arab barb like death's dark angel flew,
Great clots of angry foam clogging his bit
And spattering his black breast; his panting sides
Flayed with remorseless spurs; his nostril-pits
Swimming with blood; his red eyes mad with pain.
The couriers were lost to sight behind;
The villages fell from the way like beads
Dropped from a runner's broken rosary;
And still Haroun urged on his horse, whose feet
Devoured the way as flame consumes the straw;
Till as the third day died on Masabdan,
Before the Caliph's tent the steed fell stark,
And, heeding not, Haroun entered in haste
To kneel with death beside his father's bed.

In the tent's dusky gloom the Caliph's eyes
Shone like some tiger's tracked to her dim lair

Who fights above her cubs, fierceness and love
Blazing within them as he raised his head
And looked upon Haroun.
                           " At last," he cried,
" At last, thanks be to Allah, thou art come.
It is for thee that I set forth, and met
Death in the way; but thou at least shalt reign !"

" There is no god but Allah," said Haroun;
" Him do I fear, and Him do I obey."

Nor lest he vex the dying would deny
That which lay nearest to the Caliph's heart,
Although he would not do this wickedness.

From his wan, nerveless finger, where the damp
Of death already gathered cold, Al Mohdi drew
His signet ring, a ruby beyond price
That might have graced the crown of great Djamschid,
A well of living fires, whereon was graved
With perfect art the words which were his seal:
"ALLAH SUFFICETH ME." A camel's load
Of gold dinârs were but a petty part
Of that ring's worth, the kingdom's richest gem.

"This is the sign," murmured his ashen lips,
"Of my unbounded love, which yearns to thee,
And of thy sovereignty. Wear it, O son,
For my sake and thine own, till Asrael come
To bring thee to my side in Paradise ;
Then yield it to thine heir."
                              And when the ring,
Red as the life-blood of a hero's heart,
Slipped on the finger of Haroun, one sigh
The Caliph gave, and died out of his pain.

II

Soon as the wailing cry of Fâtima
Told those without that death had claimed her lord,
In haste the nobles gathered, eager each
To be the first to show his loyal zeal,
And greet Haroun as Caliph.
                              "Hail," they cried,
"Commander of the Faithful!   Let us know
What is thy will."
                   But he put from his lips
The sweet cup of their homage.
                                "Not to me,"
He answered, "falls the throne.   Now swear we all
Allegiance to Al Hadi."
                        And he sent
Fleet messengers to bear his brother word,
Calling him to the crown; and rested not
Until Al Hadi wore the sacred sword,
And sat upon his father's throne.
                                  And first
Al Hadi hid the hatred in his heart,
Feigning to love Haroun.   But use of power

Begot indifference to such disguise;
For all men praised the Caliph, till he went
Clad in the garment of men's glances, fed
On honey of applause, drank the strong wine
Of flattery, and felt himself a god.
Then frowningly he looked upon Haroun;
And all the courtiers from the younger turned
As bees forsake a jasmine struck with blight;
Till as the moon waned to a silver thread
Haroun walked, wearing still Al Mohdi's ring.

But ever envy dwells in courts of kings,
And sycophants like flies round honey swarm,
And malice buzz continually, and fill
A king's ears with a thousand treacherous hints;
Still bent on thrusting others down, that thus
They may themselves stand higher. So there came
One to Al Hadi on a certain day,
And said:
   "Commander of the Faithful, lo,
Lord of the world art thou, and yet the ring
Which is the signet of that sovereignty
Thy brother wears: — that ruby beyond price
Which all the wide world over is not matched;

That gem of sorcery which in its spell
Holds might to set up thrones and cast them down."

And with dark hints whose sinister design
Flashed as the quick, small lightnings come and go
When storm clouds gather, in his ear they poured
The story of Al Mohdi's love, and how
A sorcerer had to Al Mohdi sworn
That he who wore that ring should some day reign;
Till the new Caliph, mindful now no more
How on his head Haroun had set the crown,
And thinking of the son should be his heir,
Grew sick with jealousy, and heard their words
With the quick ears of hate.
      "Find this Haroun,"
He gave command; "and bring me back the ring."

Then straightway officers set forth to do
His bidding. Searching long, at last they found
Haroun, who mused upon a bridge which spanned
The Tigris, leaning on the parapet,
Watching the day and eve together melt
As bride and groom meet in a fond embrace.
Smooth lay the river as an infant's check;

The sun was gone, and all the shimmering sky
Flushed with the roseate hues in which it died
As reddens the bride's face before her lord.
The new moon faintly glimmered, and the sails
Of a black boat belated down the tide
Stretched their white shadow; while the evening star,
As if dissolving in the golden haze,
Dropped down behind the world.
                              Wrapped was Haroun
In brooding fancies, till he heeded not
How waxed or waned the restless world of men;
While they saluted with scant courtesy
As courtier metes to one from whom withdraws
The royal favor.
                "Prince Haroun," they said,
"The Caliph bids us bring that signet ring
A wizard gave thy father to ensure
His royal state."
                As if he heard them not
Haroun still watched the river, where red gleams
From the red clouds fell like spent embers, tossed
From wavelet on to wavelet till devoured
By lurking shadows. And again they spoke,
And yet again, while still he answered not;

But when at last they dared some dastard hint
Of their lord's power to take that which he would,
He turned and faced them as a lion turns
To front a jackal with consuming scorn.

"Go say unto the Caliph that the ring
My father's fingers, faltering with death,
Felt blindly with cold touch to put on mine,
No other man wears while I live. Tell him
Whom I myself set on his throne, that thus
I answer the demand which should have shamed
Either the Caliph or the brother. See!"

And as he spoke he plucked the signet off,
And flung it flashing in the dying light
As if it were a crimson fleck let fall
From the red sky, that dropped and sank down quenched
Into the bosom of the river; while
The Tigris flowed on smoothly, all unmoved
To bear the burden of one secret more.

III

Then hatred festered in the Caliph's heart,
While yet he dared not hurt Haroun, so well
The people loved him; but henceforth the prince,
Shunning the court and frowns hid in false smiles
Like poisoned blade in jewel-broidered sheath,
Walked the dim byways of retirement.

Once, on a day the stars marked fortunate,
Haroun hunted the antelope, and came
In the hot afternoon, parched with sharp thirst,
To shade of date-palms clustered round a spring.
And as he reined his horse, bidding a slave
Fill from the well his golden cup, there flew
From feathery bough a falcon yellow-eyed
To perch upon his wrist. Amazed Haroun
Looked on the bird, whose glossy neck was ringed
With golden collar turquoise-set.
                              "Some lord,"
He said, "goes seeking thee, fair falcon. None
Of all my hawks match thee in beauty fierce,
Save only one proud bird from Ispahan."

Speaking, he stretched his hand out for the cup
A slave brought brimming from the palm-fringed well;
When that strong falcon, with quick fluttering wings,
Fell on the cup, and dashed it from his hand.

"Nay, froward ranger," cried Haroun; "forbear!
Who taught thee that thou dealest with a prince
So favorless none fear to do him spite?"

But thrice the cup was filled, and thrice again
The falcon beat it empty from his grasp
Before the hunter's parching lip could taste
A single cooling drop.
                              "Now by mine eyes!"
Haroun cried; "patience poured on thee is lost
Like water wasted on the desert sand."

And with one angry sweep of his keen sword
He slew the noble hawk; but ere his hand
Could thrust the blade back in its sheath
His look fell on a damsel who advanced
Between the palm trees as an arrow flies
Straight to its mark. She was a pearl of maids,
So fair his heart burst into flame of love

Soon as his eyes beheld her beauteous face.
As straight and slender as a minaret
But supple as a reed which in the wind
Bends as it swaying waves in melting curves,
She walked, until she stood beside Haroun.

"Now was it nobly done, my lord," she said,
"To slay the falcon that had trusted thee?
Surely a hero would not wrong the faith
The helpless stayed on him; and this poor bird
Had done thee service."
                        On Haroun's swart cheek
The flush of anger faded, while his gaze
Was eloquent as verse of Hafiz.
                                "Nay,"
He said, " O moon of beauty; yet all men
May smite a traitor. I had cherished him
But that he dashed my cup down when with thirst
I perish here."
                "Bid now thy servants see,"
The damsel answered, "what lies in the well."

She drew a step back, and with scornful eyes
Stood waiting till the frightened slaves made search,

And came again to fall down at his feet,
Crying:
    "O lord and master, pardon! Lo,
Hid in the well a mangled serpent lies,
Whose venom taints the water."
        "O rash prince,
O prince ungrateful," that fair damsel said,
"Had not my falcon better watched thy life
Than these thy slaves, thou wert in Paradise!"

"There is no god but Allah," swift Haroun
Made answer; "and in Paradise I am
Since I am where thou art, O houri-faced, —
Who cannot but be one of those sweet maids
Whom Allah gives to heroes after death."

"My lord," she answered, "I am but a maid
Of humble hill folk; my dead father's hawk
Flew from my hand as I stood by my tent,
And led me, following, down into the plain
To meet my lord, that so this bird was slain,
And I left falconless."
    "Nay," said Haroun,
"Take of my hawks the finest, even this,

The falcon beyond price, with breast of snow
And eyes of fire, brought from far Ispahan.
Tell me thy name, I pray thee, peri-eyed,
That when men ask who is the fairest maid
Of all earth's daughters, I may make reply."

"Thy hand-maid is Siatrah called," she said,
Her voice as soft as crooning of the dove
When first her nestlings burst the shell. "Behold,
Fierce are the fervors of the afternoon,
And my lord thirsts. Ride but to yonder hill,
And there be tents for shelter from the sun,
And sherbets cooled with snow."
                                So to the hills
Haroun rode with his train, and in her tent,
Reclining on fair cushions, soft as clouds,
Drank sherbets icy cool, but deeper draughts
Of the hot wine of love. To her sweet lute,
From which the notes dropped as the liquid myrrh
Drips from the wounded tree-trunk, low she sang,
While her large eyes beseeching seemed to plead
Forgiveness for the boldness of her song:

>"With eyes of fire the falcon flew,
>   To dash the poison from his hand;

The guerdon of that service true,
  Was the swift death-stroke of his brand.
Ah, hapless bird, who can deny
That love's last proof is still to die!

"The maid to save her falcon sped,
  And heard his words of honeyed phrase,
Like drops of fragrant balsam shed,
  Or wooing warbler's melting lays.
Ah, maid, beware! All prayers deny;
Lest love call thee in proof to die!"

"Now, nay," Haroun cried; "trust thou nought save love!
Love is not love that does not long to serve.
Love shall defend thee, whoso would assail;
Love be thy slave to do thy lightest hest;
Love shall be stanch even in face of death;
And love attend thy way to Paradise!"

Then from her slender hand he caught the lute,
And sang, his looks with longing eloquent:

"As in waves beyond number the sea
  Beats still in immortal unrest,

So ever with yearning for thee,
    The swelling heart throbs in my breast.

"As the moon keeps its course all unmoved
    However the ocean may sway,
So thou, with thy heart yet unproved,
    Goest calm on thy beauteous way.

"O thou moon of desire, on me
    With kindlier glance look thou down;
Draw me up like a flame unto thee,
    Let my soul in thy radiance drown!"

Thus through the brief-long moments wonderful
They held bewitching converse, while the day
Waned down the west until the sunset flamed
With crimson fires, like rubies beyond price
Spilled from the hand of some affrighted djinn
In frantic flight for life. Then through the dusk,
Fragrant with camphor scents and breath of rose,
And laced with luscious songs of nightingales
Like a fair mead with silver streams, Haroun
Rode back to Bagdad, — but without his heart!

IV

Thenceforward well the courser of Haroun
Knew the road to Siatrah's dwelling. Fleet
As her slain falcon sped he on his way,
Swift as the wind, while yet Haroun's fond thought
Outsped him in his flight. Great was the love
Between Siatrah and Haroun; so great
It justified all woes that earth has known.
Their hearts like twin drops melted into one,
While joy filled their souls full as sunlight fills
The golden globes of dew when morning breaks.

But who is loved by one is loved by two;
And she whom one desires stirs other hearts.
Fairest of all the daughters of her race,
Radiant in her world-troubling loveliness,
Siatrah walked, while measureless desire
Burned in the breast of whoso looked on her.
No man beheld her but to be her slave,
No youth of all the hill-folk but adored,
Though none save one dare lift his eyes in hope
Up to her height of peerless queenliness.

Warrior and chieftain of the tribe, Kareem
Was like a star of fire in cloud-strewn skies,
Baleful and red, of presage sinister,
Bodeful of tempests and world-sweeping wars.
Long had he loved Siatrah.   She alone
Could tame his fierceness though she mocked his love
With teasing word and witchery of smiles
Which bound him faster still in the meshed net
Of her enchantments.

     Wroth to madness waxed
Kareem when all the gossips of the tribe
Chattered of the hot wooing of Haroun.
Some while his rage smouldered like hidden coals
Under heaped ashes; then at last broke forth
As when the night wind blows among the tents
And fans to life the embers seeming dead.
His pleading to Siatrah ran to waste
Like water poured in vessels bottomless.
Ever she met his prayers with one same word:

" Since every other damsel of our tribe
Waits like fruit over-ripe thy plucking hand,
Why fret thy heart with wasted love for me?

Thou wast kind to my father, O Kareem;
Therefore I pray let no unfriendliness
Between us wrong his memory; but since
Allah hath left my heart of love for thee
Barren as is the desert of the rose,
Vex me no more with importunings vain!"

So, mad with anger and the stinging smart
Of passion unrequited, to the plain
Where lay the road to Bagdad rode Kareem,
Through thickets of pomegranate trees whose blooms
Gleamed out like stars of fire in emerald seas,
Seeking his rival in the bosky ways;
And came upon him just beneath the palms
Beside the well, where first Haroun had seen
The world-enhancing beauty of his love.

Like the black face of Eblis was the face
Kareem turned on Haroun, reining his horse
Close to his very bridle. His wrath swept
Like the death-dealing sand-storm of the waste
Where bones lie bleached and the air seethes with thirst.
His curses fell upon Haroun as kites
Fall on their prey to rend it. His keen tongue

Was as a thistle to the naked foot.
Long time Haroun with patience suffered him,
Knowing his kindness to Siatrah's kin;
Till at the last his insolence broke down
All patience as a mountain torrent fierce,
Swollen with rain, bursts through a barrier.
Stung by the fury of his beating words,
Haroun unloosed the bands of speech, and cried:

"Mayst thou be stung by scorpions of Cashan!
Thine is a soul that swarms with evil thoughts
As slime-pits swarm with serpents! Now no more
Profane her honor-giving name and mine
With thy foul leprosy of words; but draw
Thy sword!"

          He leaped down lightly from his horse,
An Arab barb white as the foam on milk,
And stood clad in his rage as in linked mail,
While his jade-hafted blade flashed in the sun.

As when a leopard at a lion leaps,
A whirlwind of incarnate rage, so dashed
Kareem, foaming with wrath, against Haroun;
But unabashed as a great eagle were

If fierce against it flew a sparrow-hawk,
Haroun withstood his blows and beat him back.
As when one stamps a dying watch-fire out,
The sparks flew from their flashing swords, which rang
Like cymbals smitten when tribes rush to war.
Their horses, with distended nostrils, neighed
In keen delight of battle, while in fear
The timid lizards fled their trampling feet.

But not for long might one withstand Haroun,
Whose sword was like the name of Solomon.
He smote the chieftain of the hill-folk down,
And stood above him proud and terrible,
In strength and beauty like the wild white ass,
Tempered like a Damascus blade of price,
A prince of men, worthy Siatrah's grace.

"Live," said Haroun, "since her dead father's love
Hath made thee sacred."
      But before Kareem
Could rise or answer, there beside them stood
Siatrah, with her heart-bewildering face.

"Lo, thus," she cried, "our chief betrays the guest
Bound to our tribe by covenant of salt!

I smote the slave who told me in the plain
Thou wouldst waylay my lord; what then is meet
That I should do to thee who prove him true?"

And cut to heart Kareem abased his face,
Groaning in agony of rage and shame.
Then raised his head to cry with bitter tongue:

"What is the covenant of salt to him
Whose heart's delight is stolen? Not my guest
Is he who steals my love, although there be
A thousand vows between us! Oh, dove-eyed,
How shall I win thee? What price buys thy heart?
See! Though we be but hill-folk, I can give
Brocades and slaves and carpets from far Ind,
And strings of amber beads, and cups of gold,
Turquoise and coral, and great jewels red
Our fathers won as spoil of rich Iran."

Then she smiled on him till between her lips
Her white teeth shone like hailstones fallen between
The crimson petals of a rose; and turned
To flash upon him mocking eyes, and say:

"The only jewel that could buy my love
Is that ring which Haroun, as all men know,

Flung in the Tigris. When thou bringest that
My love requites thee!"

       Then Kareem leaped up,
His blood-shot eyes on fire with passion wild,
And cast upon the twain a burning look
Like baleful spell of sorcery accursed.

"So be it!" through clenched teeth he said. "I go
To win thy dower from the Tigris' bed."

And mounting his black horse, he rode away
Across the plain to where the minarets
Of Bagdad showed against the sunset sky.

V

Well nigh unto its end wore Ramadhan,
The weary, wasting moon of penitence,
Wherein from dawn till sunset all men fast.
Only one day there was, left like a leaf
Withered and fluttering on the bough forlorn.
And on the eve of that last day, elate
With knowledge of the coming of her love,
Siatrah robed herself in lustrous silk
In hue like a ripe fig, purple at once
And green, and yet not either; wrought with gold
And richest tracery of needlework;
While here and there were clasps with sapphires set
And rubies red as sunbeams plunged in wine.
On yielding cushions languidly reclined
She waited her lord's coming, her full heart
Aching with rapture as a mother's breast
Strains, full and round, to her babe's nursing lip.
Musk, myrrh, and camphor, sandal-wood and spice,
Perfumed the air about her; while the tent
Glowed with the light of clustered silver lamps
Fed with sweet-scented oils.   Slave girls unseen

With soft, persuasive fingers touched the lute
In melting cadences voluptuous,
Or breathed melodious sighs through low-voiced
    pipes;
Till, joining in their strain, Siatrah sang:

  "Oh, love, thou art freer than breath!
  Oh, love, thou art fiercer than hate!
  Oh, love, thou art stronger than death!
  Oh, love, thou art mightier than fate!
  From the touch of thy hand who can flee?
  At the sound of thy voice who can stay?
  Who can measure his strength against thee?
  If thou askest for life, say thee nay?"

And even as she sang, a slave girl fell,
Panting with haste and fear, before her feet;
And had but time to cry one word — "Kareem!" —
Before the chief put the tent-curtain by,
And stood before her, his fierce, cruel eyes
Like eyes of tiger with claws buried deep
In his prey's side.
              "O jasmine-tree," he said,
"Cast in the mold of comeliness, and framed

To tease the hearts of men, when shall be set
Our bridal feast? For, lo! I bring thee here
The ring which is thy heart's desire."

                                          He held
The great red ruby, quick with splendid fires,
Like a torch to Siatrah; but she shrank
As if its redness were a serpent's mouth.

"Allah is most compassionate!" she cried;
"It cannot be that thou hast found the ring!"

Her lips were pallid, and she shook with fear
As a frail harebell on a torrent's marge
Trembles with the near passion of the stream.

"Allah is most compassionate!" cried back
Kareem. "He knoweth that thou art to me
As water unto him who dies of thirst;
As sight unto the blind; fire to the torch;
Or light unto the day, which lacking it
Were darksome night! Therefore hath Allah wrought
A miracle to save me, that I win
Haroun's lost ring, which is thy beauty's price."

Unseen the minstrel slave girls still played on
Their joyous music, but Siatrah's joy
Was as a light put out.
                       "Tell me," she said,
Her words faltering like mourners blind with tears,
"This miracle that hath been wrought for thee."

"Eight days," he said, "I sent the divers down,
And made the fishers drag their nets in search
Of this great signet of Al Mohdi. Deep
They dived, and crawled like crawfish in the ooze;
But found it not; and at the last despair
Took hold upon my heart like frosts that chill
The tender blossoms of the almond tree.
But on the ninth day came a sorcerer,
Lean as a lance-staff, withered, brown and dry
As locust-pod, with snow-white beard which fell
Below his girdle. 'Cast the net,' he said,
'There where the farthest shadow of the bridge
Falls when the voice of the muezzin cries
The hour of noonday prayer.' And by mine eyes!
When there the cast was made, it brought the ring
Up from the flood tangled in the net's mesh.
It is thy dower, and thou art mine at last!"

But she drew back, and thrust the ring aside.

"I love thee not, and I am not for thee,"
She said. "Take comfort in the price Haroun
Will pay thee for the ring."
      "Now by my beard,"
He cried in bitter rage; "is this thy faith?
When did thy father's daughter learn to wear
The robe of falsehood? Thou thyself didst make
This ring thy dower!"
     Then with cruel words
Which stung her quivering soul like nine-thonged lash
That tears with bloody stripes a slave's bared back
He railed upon her, while she had no word
Save that in mockery she named the ring;
Until at last her sudden rage leaped up
And quenched out all forbearance utterly
As an armed warrior's heel stamps out a spark.

"Begone!" she cried. "Lest I should call my slaves
To cast thee forth!"
     "To-morrow I will come,"
He answered her in taunt, "with sound of flutes
And drums and cymbals and with dancing girls,

To set thee on a tall white camel's back
And bear thee far away from Bagdad. Lo,
Now thou art mine, I will not thou shouldst yield
Fair looks and gracious words to this Haroun.
This outcast brother of the Caliph comes
Too often to thy tent! Thou art a grape
For other mouth than his! Give him no more
The smile of welcome."

       Blown with insolence
As a puff-adder with its venom, sure
He held her fast, he gloated on her pain;
But she flashed on him such a look of scorn
That he was like a bubble burst. He turned
And laid his hand on the tent-curtain.

           "Yea,"
He said, "to-morrow I will come!"

           But when
The curtain fell behind him, wan and pale
As the gray ashes on a burned-out brand,
Reeling with grief as she were drunk with wine,
Siatrah rose as she would follow him;
But heard through the night noises and the sound
Of sweet, smooth melodies the slave girls played,
The beating of a horse's hoofs, and knew

Haroun drew near. Straightway she smiled again,
Drawing the mantle of concealment o'er
The anguish of her breast; for though her pain
Strike with its serpent-fangs her very heart,
A woman hides her woe from him she loves,
Lest he be grieved in seeing. Sad at soul
Siatrah wore the guise of joyousness
As bride unwilling wears the marriage robe.

VI

But when Haroun put the tent curtain by,
As the moon puts aside a cloud, his brow
Was dark with shadow of perplexity;
And though his eyes gladdened at sight of her
Like pools on which the sudden sunlight falls,
Her heart divined some trouble in his breast.
So from her lips she scattered pearls of speech,
Comforting him, and when at last he smiled,
She kissed his hand, and said:
 "Tell me, my lord,
What trouble casts its cloud upon thy face.
If it must be I may not cure thy grief
At least together we will bear its pain,
That so the time seem shorter till it flee;
For sorrow, risen like the morning sun,
Yet like the sun must set."
 And with a kiss
Brimming with love as rose-cups with perfume,
Haroun made answer, fondling her slim hand.

"At sunset," said he, "while my fond heart ached
With thirst for thee, after the long day's fast,

I rode out at the city's gate, as full
Of joy as is a burning torch with light;
When met me in the way a sorcerer,
Lean as a lance-staff, brown as camel's heel,
With beard that hid his girdle, and with eyes
Which pierced me like a sword-prick. 'Lo, Haroun,'
He cried as if in menace terrible,
'Where is that ring thy dying father gave
In sign that thou shouldst sit upon his throne?
To-morrow ends the fast of Ramadhan,
And who to-morrow wears that fateful ring
Shall reign as Caliph when the stars shall rise.'
He cast on me a look of threat and blame,
But yet of promise; then the place he filled
Was vacant of him; and across the plain
I sped to thee. But that old sorcerer
Seemed still to hold my bridle, while his eyes
Said things inscrutable and full of fate."

Pale was Siatrah, but she took his hand,
And round his finger wound a shining tress
Of her long hair, black as a falcon's neck,
Murmuring with laughter:
                    "What more precious ring
Can my lord long for, having this?"

                                            And he
Warmed it with fervent kisses, crying out:

"What care I to be Caliph, since thine heart,
The only kingdom I desire, is mine!"

So had they joy in love until Haroun
Was comforted; but when the feast was brought, —
Cheeses and wheaten cakes, and snowy curds,
With meats pistachio-stuffed, and luscious dates,
Quinces in flavor like wine mixed with musk,
Melons as pink as young girls' cheeks, with seeds
Black as their eyes, and sherbets cooled with snow, —
Siatrah slipped aside, and whispered to a slave:

"Haste to Kareem, and bid him send the ring.
Say that to-morrow I will pay the price."

Then, when the feast was done, she sang this lay,
Which from her lips in wooing accents fell
Like silver bells heard far off in the night,
While mingled with its melting cadences
The sweet, melodious trouble of her lute:

> "Dear love, when in thine arms I lie,
>   And feel thy faithful heart

Throbbing with love which cannot die,
    And know how true thou art, —
Ah, why unbidden to mine eyes
Should foolish teardrops thronging rise?
    Why should I weep?

"Dear love, thy kiss falls on my mouth,
    Thine arms hold me again;
I drink thy looks as earth in drouth
    Drinks drops of welcome rain;
Once more upon thine ardent breast
My glowing cheeks are hidden pressed;
    And yet I weep.

"When thou art gone, and I am lone,
    Bereft of life in thee,
When all this joy which we have known
    Lost in the past shall be; —
Then, when undone by sorrow's ache,
In death my heart shall refuge take;
    I shall not weep!"

With bosom swelling like a moonlit wave
She cast the lute aside, and flung her arms,

Twin miracles of matchless loveliness,
About Haroun, weeping upon his breast.
Then as a mother soothes a child at night
Frightened by some dream afrit-sent, Haroun
With soft endearments dried her blinding tears;
And when her sobs were done, took up the lute,
In his turn singing verse fragrant with love:

"Was I not thine when Allah spoke the word
    Which formed from smoke the sky?
  Were not our twin hearts one when heaven heard
    The first faint stars reply?

"Canst thou then doubt that while the ages roll
    Our being one shall be?
  As flame and light are one, so is my soul
    One, O my love, with thee!

"The ebbing star-floods of the Judgment Day
    Shall leave my heart still thine;
  And Paradise itself shall fade away
    Ere I thy love resign!"

Thus like two tamarisk-haunting turtle-doves
They joyed together till the wasting night

Called him away; and when she said farewell,
She gave into his hand a casket sealed,
Bidding him open it when day should come,
And the muezzin called to morning prayer.

Then when his horse's hoof-beats died away,
She hid no longer her heart-burning grief;
But from her hand she loosed the cord of hope,
And sank into the whirlpool of despair.

VII

On that last day of Ramadhan there came
Unto Al Hadi those who said:
                              "Haroun
Plots with the hill-folk, and will rouse the tribes
To swarm on Bagdad like the ants which come
Where grains of wheat are scattered; on their spears
His treason rides unto thy throne."
                                    And he,
Hating Haroun, and thinking how he stood
Between the crown and that son whom he loved,
Swore by his beard the shadow of Haroun
Should fall no longer on the whole wide earth;
And gave command to Hârthamah, the chief
Of all his trusted guards, to rid him swift
Of this his fear.
                 But swiftly from her place
Behind the women's lattice, where she heard,
Khizâran, mother of them both, broke forth,
And cast herself before Al Hadi's feet.

"Who slays my son, slays me!" she cried. "Haroun
Is as thou art, O son, blood of my blood,

Flesh of my flesh, bone of my very bone!
Let not this thing be done in Allah's sight,
Lest He should curse thee with the curse of Cain!"

But from her frenzied grasp he drew his robe,
And answered her with anger:
       "Well I know
That thou wouldst rather have me slain! Too long
Haroun hath been as sand within mine eye.
Get back unto thy distaff; meddle not
With high concerns of state."
       Yet still she prayed,
Beating her aged breast as the wave beats
On the hoar sand, and weeping sore.
       "O son,
Whom these same breasts have suckled, I am old, —
If thou must needs have blood, take mine, since he
Is what my hand hath made him! Mine the blame
If he offend thee! Hurt not his sweet life
Who is the jewel on thy people's brow,
The noblest man Allah hath made!"
       She turned
And fixed on Hârthamah her blazing eyes.

"In the great Day of Fear," she cried, "will I,
Even at Allah's very throne, demand
The blood of this my son Haroun!"
            And he,
Awed by her fury, would have joined her plea
But that Al Hadi, lest he choke with rage,
Left the divan, and sought the women's court,
Belching forth curses blistering to the ears;
While after him Khizâran followed, pale,
And tottering like one with blindness struck.

"Give me to drink," Al Hadi cried. "Are all
In league with that black son of hell, Haroun,
That ye would have me strangle here with thirst?"

As fields of growing wheat bend to a storm,
Before his anger all the slave girls bowed,
Mute and amazed, daring not answer him;
Smitten with horror at the sacrilege
That one should drink in sacred Ramadhan;
While his wives pleaded:
         "Break thou not the fast,
Commander of the Faithful, lest a curse
Fall on thee!"

    But from old Khizâran's eyes
There flashed a look was like the lightning's gleam.

"Thou shalt have drink," she answered. "Ease thine
   heart
With that which I shall give thee, and forgive
That I have dared rebel at thy decree,
When thou art Caliph as thou art my son."

Then, though the time was holy Ramadhan,
She brought him sherbet cooled with mountain snow,
Acid with citron, fragrant with sweet musk,
Enticing to the sense.
      But as he drank
Sudden death clutched the Caliph unaware,
Its bony fingers closing on his throat.

A burst of fear and horror rose from all
The frightened women, as sharp tumult rings
From smitten armor when an ambush leaps
Upon its prey; while after Hârthamah,
Who in the palace court marshalled his troop,
Her gray hair streaming wild and her fierce eyes
Like watch-fire coals at night, Khizâran sped,

Shrieking:
              "Go not! Allah hath smitten him
Who would have smitten! Not death for Haroun,
But that throne which his dying father gave!"

And like a ghoul she triumphed, while within
The voice of wailing mourned her first-born son.

Well had Khizâran loved Haroun, at heart
Hating Al Hadi that he wore the crown;
And through the palace ran, pursuing swift
The tidings of the Caliph's death as hound
Follows a hare, the whisper that her hand
Had with a subtle poison slain the son
She hated, that the one she loved might live.
Like a wild wind throughout the palace swept
Fright and uncertainty tumultuous;
While all the courtiers, dazed with dread and doubt,
Questioned to whom their homage should be paid.
Bagdad buzzed like a hive when wanton boys
Rifle its honey; and "Haroun! Haroun!"
The people cried, raising his name on high
As it had been the standard of a host.

Then took Khizâran trusty messengers,
And sent them forth as if they fled from flame.

"Faster than fear," she cried, "fleet to Haroun;
Bid him to haste before the throne be cold!"

But Hârthamah to cunning council called
Those who had been Al Hadi's creatures.
                                                 "See,"
He said; "fate gives the lot into our hands.
If on the throne we set Al Hadi's son,
This boy scarce yet out of his mother's arms,
We reign through him, using his name to be
Only the shield behind which hides our will."

So in the web of destiny the threads
Of death and fear and hope and hate and love
Were mingled, as the tireless hand of Fate
Threw the remorseless shuttle, for Haroun
Weaving the robe of sovereignty at last.

VIII

On that last sacred day of Ramadhan
It needed not the call to sunrise prayer
To rouse Haroun from dreams in which his hand
Yet felt Siatrah's fingers warm in his,
In which he thrilled with fervor of her kiss
As thrills the moth which drowns itself in flame.
Soon as the morning prayer was said, he took
The casket which Siatrah gave, and kissed,
And tore away its silken wrappings, broke
The clasps inlaid with coral, — and aghast
Saw shine before his eyes Al Mohdi's ring.

It seemed some wild, fantastic sorcery,
But on the ruby red as his heart's blood
He saw the sacred name, and read once more
Al Mohdi's seal: "ALLAH SUFFICETH ME."
He bit the finger of amazement, lost
In baffled wonder how the jewel came
Unto Siatrah's hand; then eager sped
To take his curd-white horse in haste to ride
Up to the hills and her.

                        But in the gate
Sat that weird sorcerer, snow-bearded, brown,
And lean as an old gossip's spindle.
                                        "Stay,
Commander of the Faithful," was the word
He breathed into Haroun's astonished ear.
"Go not from Bagdad till the sun be set.
Thou hast the ring I to thy father gave, —
The ring of doom.   This is the day of fate."

"Commander of the Faithful am I not,"
Haroun said; "but his brother favorless,
Like some poor vessel scorned contemptuously
And cast aside, which yet he dare not break
Because the Bagdad folk have loved me well
As well they loved my father, — on whom peace!"

The other answered not, but took his rein,
And turned the white steed quickly in the gate,
And waved Haroun the way that he should go
Back to his dwelling.   There the long hours through
Haroun mused on his fate and of the ring,
Lost in a thicket of perplexity
So dense and thorny he might not escape;

Until at last Khizâran's messengers
Burst in upon his musings with wide eyes
Bloodshot with haste, and panting breath, to cry:

"Commander of the Faithful, we are come
To bring thee to thy throne. Pray thee, arise,
And come with haste, lest treason in thy place
Should set another."   But Haroun broke forth,
Smitten with deep amazement:
                            "Lo, what snare
Spreads now my brother for my feet, that ye
Are sent with mouths as full of lies as breath
To fool me into treason?"
                            But they said,
Abasing reverent foreheads to the dust:

"There is no God save Allah. At His word
Hath Asrael slain thy brother."
                            And they showed
All that was done, and how Khizâran sent
To speed his coming; till Haroun arose,
And hastened through the streets, hearing his name
Thrown on from voice to voice as men might fling

Their turbans up, inebriate with joy.
So came they to the secret door where gray,
Consumed with shivering fear and burning hope,
Khizâran crouched in waiting.
                              "O my son,
Light of mine eyes, bliss-bringer!" fierce she cried;
And kissed his forehead and his mouth, and wept
Upon his hands, delirious with joy.
"Now thou art Caliph! Now the morn is come
After the bitter blackness of my night!
Now the sun rises, and my withered age
Is turned to verdant youth!"
                              But he put by
Her glowing words, which spilled their gladness forth
As a ripe sun-warmed grape oozes its juice.
An instant he stood silent, while she hushed
Her cry of clamorous rejoicing, awed
By the accusing question of his eyes.

"Thou art my mother," said he, "but thou wert
His mother too; hast thou then given death
To him who in thy bosom first knew life?"

But she bent on him eyes inscrutable,
Like polished ebony, and cried in scorn:

"Do I give life and death? By Allah's hand,
And by His hand alone, the lot of life
Or death is cast for all. Thy brother sinned,
Breaking the fast of holy Ramadhan,
And Allah smote him. — Let the dead be dead!"

Nor would she stay for further questioning,
But thrust into his hand a cimeter,
Curved like the eyelash of his love, and cried:

"Lo, while thou lingerest here, in yonder room
Is thy throne sold as if in the bazaar
A merchant sold a carpet!"
                          Through the gloom
Of secret passages she led him on
Until he stood within a curtained niche,
And heard the voice of Hârthamah, who said:

"So shall all power be ours, and proud Haroun
Shall die as was commanded. In the name
Of this boy Caliph may we work our will
Till we have bent this people to our sway
As the strong bowman bends the stubborn bow;

While this Haroun shall be as yesterday
That is forgotten."
                        But one courtier said,
Craft and reluctance mingling in his tone
As two snakes writhe together in the slime:

"Nay, be not rash, lest in the Day of Fear
Allah shall hurl thee howling down to hell
To everlasting torment. We have sworn
Unto Al Mohdi, when in Masabdan
Dying he lay, that we would serve Haroun,
Binding our vow with oaths so terrible
Even the djinns accurs'd would keep such oath."

"Now, nay," another said: "by Allah's eyes
We swore our faith to him who wore the ring
Which was Al Mohdi's signet. Since Haroun
Hath flung that in the Tigris, we are free,
And our oath binds us not."
                         Then swift Haroun
Put by the curtain, and before them stood.
Upon his clenched left hand upraised, the ring
Blazed like an angry afrit's eye. His right
Held with firm grasp the keen-edged cimeter,

While his face shone with fire of majesty
Consumed resistance as flame shrivels tow.

"Nay, by the Prophet's beard," he said, "not so!
Allah hath sent the signet back to me.
The ring is here, and here your Caliph stands!
I would not that this day auspicious be
A day of death, but by my father's ring
I swear that ye who plot in secret here
Like rats that undermine a lofty wall,
Shall yield allegiance, or this cimeter
Shall drink your blood as gluttons drink red wine!"

As when a falcon falls upon a flock
Of timorous rock-doves, and so great their fright
They dare not even flee, so stood Haroun
Amid the cowering courtiers stricken mute
With fear and baffled hate.
                      "Behold!" they cried,
"Allah indeed hath wrought a miracle,
And brought the signet from the Tigris' depths.
Vain were it to contend with Allah's might.
Since He hath spoken, let His will be done."

And soon all Bagdad rang like a struck drum,
Reverberating with the name "Haroun!"
Proclaimed Commander of the Faithful, named
Caliph of Kings from every minaret.

IX

But when the sun went down, and Ramadhan
Was done, and the clear stars rose on Haroun
And found him Caliph; when the whole land rang
With festal songs and joy of many feasts
And all the clanging din of revelry;
When torches made the sky of night to glow
Like a bride's cheek; and dead Al Hadi lay
Like a past fear forgotten; then Haroun
Stole from the palace as a dew-drop slips
Unseen from out the bosom of a rose,
And left all pomp to hasten to his love.

Across the plains up to the well loved hills
His white steed took the old familiar way,
While night darkened around and faint winds rose
To toss the palm-trees' plumy tops and moan
Through the acacia thickets. Weird and high,
Like famine-dizzy camels, the gray clouds
Wandered about the sky, fantastic shapes;
While in the air were presages of ill
As evil spirits foul beset his way.

But wrapped in love dreams sweet, and heeding not
If it were night or day, Haroun spurred on,
Soft murmuring to himself as if his love
Already heard him:
     "Heart-inflaming one,
O wonder-maid, bewildering eyes and soul,
How long the moments while I stay from thee,
How brief the hours while I am by thy side!
Now that the throne is mine, thy place shall be
No longer in the tents, like some rich gem
Left all unset; thy glorious light shall shine
In Bagdad's proudest palace, like a torch
Set on the city wall!"
     But as he neared
Siatrah's dwelling, on his ear there fell
The voices of sad women wailing sore,
While ever moaning rebecs teased the ear
Repeating one insistent note of pain;
And like a shaft which from an ambush flies,
A keen and sudden terror pierced his breast.
He drew his rein as if to stay his horse,
Then struck the spurs into its side, and dashed
Up to the tent dim-lighted whence welled forth
The woeful anguish of that song of death.

But with his hand on the tent-curtain, faint
With fear and fore-seen agony, he paused
And heard the women sing, while rebecs plained,
The low, melodious requiem for the dead:

"The sun hath been quenched, the moon is put out,
    The stars shine no more in the sky;
Love no longer is sweet, faith is swallowed by doubt,
    Since she who was loveliest could die!"

Then he could bear no more, but flung aside
The goats'-hair curtain, and before him lay
On a long couch beneath the silver lamps
That which had been Siatrah.
                With a cry
Of awful woe which pierced to Allah's throne,
He flung him down, smitten as with a spear;
But ere his passion could find word, there rose
A clamor which broke through the women's wails;
And like a madman rushed the chief Kareem
Into that tent of death.
                Haroun sprang up,
And the two chieftains one another faced
Like snarling tigers fighting for one mate;

While all the singing women shrieked in fear,
And every rebec ceased with jarring note.

"It was for thee she died!" burst forth Kareem.
"She bought thy ring with promise of her love,
Then slew herself that she might still be thine.
Mayst thou through all eternity be shod
With shoes of fire; the Judgment Angels smite
Their iron maces on thy deathless head;
Thy brain boil in thy skull as boils a pot,
In hell whither my sword shall send thee swift!"

As a flail whistles on the waiting wheat,
His sword sang in the air, but like a flame
Waved by the wind the Caliph stepped aside,
Drawing his cimeter. With one great stroke,
In which he poured his passion and his rage
As if he struck at Asrael's very self
Avenging his love's death, he laid Kareem
Dead at the dead Siatrah's feet.
                          "Ah, woe!
Happy thou who canst die!" he groaned. "Alas!
I must live on and on and on and on!"

Then rose a woman from that weeping band,
And showed him how Siatrah's fingers, cold
And pallid from the clasp of death, enclosed
A parchment, touching his name on it writ
As if they knew and loved each syllable.
He flung to earth his bloody sword, which rang
Against the fallen blade of dead Kareem,
And took the scroll, and read through blinding tears:

"Commander of the Faithful, though thou be
Sovereign of sovereigns, oh, forget not her
Who died to have thee so, and dying felt
Death's stroke as if it were thy blissful kiss
Because she died for thee! In Paradise
She waiteth lonely till the time shall come
When thou again shalt put thy hand in hers,
And Allah, looking on her joy, shall say:
'Lo, here is bliss perfect as is mine own!'"

Then all the anguish of his heart broke forth.
He cast himself again upon the earth
Beside the couch where she who loved him lay
With breast unquickened though he came so near;

And kissed with tears the ring that was her price,
And on it read "ALLAH SUFFICETH ME."
Then cried in sudden ecstasy of woe:

"What can suffice a heart bereft of love!"

THE VOICE OF SAKINA.

THE VOICE OF SAKINA.

I

THE whole wide desert for a moment glowed
  In glory of a haze of golden light;
Then there was no more day, but the clear stars
Clustered as thick as eager bees which storm
Acacia thickets heaped with yellow bloom.
The flickering fires of the caravan
Trembled in the still air from their own breath;
The weary camels crouched beside the tents;
And one day's march less lay between the train
And Bagdad, where its journey should have end.

Precious the treasure which the caravan
Guarded across the desert. There had come
Unto the Caliph trusty messengers
From far-off Kandahar to bear him word
How a world's wonder had arisen; how

A maid more beautiful than mountain rill
To him who dies of thirst, more passing fair
Than those heart-troubling houris who pour wine
In Paradise for heroes after death;
A sweet Circassian slave, formed as of light,
A merchant there had bought with all the wealth
His hand could bring together; and he prayed
The Caliph take her for his own, since none
Save the Commander of the Faithful were
Worthy of so much beauty.   Though the price
Was that of twenty villages, not long
The Caliph doubted; but he sent Zobeir,
The captain of his guard, a man of worth,
To bring the maid to Bagdad.
                              Proud of port
Was young Zobeir, like a slim cedar-tree
Which springs upon the mountains of Iran.
Love had not touched him, but ambition's flame
Glowed hotly in his breast.   His sword alone
Was mistress of his heart; and with light scorn
He laughed adown the winds the wiles of love.
His loyalty was as a gem unflawed;
His courage as the splendor of the sun;
His truth unfailing as the dew of night.

Among the tents Zobeir walked forth alone
To see that all was well; and as he stood
Beside the tent wherein the women were,
He heard the sound of voices as one hears
The doves that coo and chatter in their cote,
With tinkle of sweet lutes, whose silver strings
Cried out with joy at the caressing touch
Of fingers fair.   Then one heart-melting tone
Rose 'mid the other voices as a thread
Of yellow gold gleams in the broideries
A princess weaves with cunning handiwork.
Quick were all others hushed, while that voice sang
Enchantments of bewitching melody.

> "In mead where roses bloom
>   I saw a withered rose.
>   'Ah!' sighed I, 'how hath doom
>   Struck thee, as love's fierce woes
>   Have blighted my sad heart,
>   Faint with their bitter smart?'
>
> "'I dreamed,' the rose replied,
>   'My nightingale was near;
>   Morn waked me, and denied
>   That dream's beguilement dear.

>   Bereft and lone, I die,
>   Since love no more is nigh.'
>
> "'Alas, poor rose!' I wept;
>   'Thy lot and mine are one.
> Joy found me while I slept,
>   But fled when sleep was done.
> Why could not morn delay
> Until the Judgment Day!'"

Then in the dimness of the night, Zobeir
Lingered entranced, and listened to that song,
While love sprang on him as a lion leaps
Out of the covert on a doe which drinks
At some lone pool. In one swift instant fled
His life's ambitions, till he had no thought
Save of the singer. Naught in all the earth
To him seemed worth the getting save a kiss
From those dear lips unseen which sang so sweet.
He dreamed no more of place or power or fame;
But under the thick clustering stars he stood,
And trembled with the thrill of new-born love.

Then when the song was done, and once again
With broken words and laughter all the air

Was filled, as when a sudden breeze shakes down
A cloud of petals from the almond-tree,
Zobeir beheld an aged slave who came
Like a dim shadow from the women's tent,
And called her to his side.
                          "Tell me," he said,
"What voice was that which sang?"
                                  The slave abased
Her forehead at his feet, and answered him:

"It is the voice which this side Paradise
Is matchless, O my lord. Sakina sang,
That pearl beyond all price for whose sweet sake
The Caliph — on whom peace! — hath sent my lord
Across the desert with this caravan."

Mute stood Zobeir, struck to the very heart,
Pierced as with stinging arrows by the thought
That not for him was she, nightingale-voiced,
But even love for her were treachery.
Within his tent that night he stricken lay,
Consumed with love and sorrow. On his head
He sprinkled bitter ashes of remorse;
And then defiant held his love on high
As if it were a sword.

"Oh, hapless fate,"
He groaned; "oh, cunning snare which Eblis sets
To catch my soul. Alas! Thou sweet-voiced one
The stars upon the heaven spell thy name,
The wind through every land goes seeking thee,
The night brings hush and darkness that thou sleep,
Day lights the earth that thou shouldst smile again,
The birds sing to thee, and the flowers bloom
And pour their fragrance forth for none save thee;
All things else serve and love thee; I alone
May love thee not! But I will love thee, sweet!
I needs must love thee as the sun must burn,
The thunder-bolt must fall! Thou wert mine own
When Allah formed us both; and I have lived
But since I heard thy voice. The thing I was
Might be the Caliph's slave, but thou hast called
A new Zobeir to being, and henceforth
That which thou hast created is thine own!
And yet — and yet — I were not worthy thee
If I were false to him!"

And drunk with pain
As with a poisoned wine, he grovelled there
While the night lapsed, and the thick stars on high
Moved slowly westward, grieving at his woe.

II

Suddenly on his ear there broke a sound
Which called him back from whirling deeps of doubt.
A cry broke through the quiet of the camp
As if some jar had clashing thrown to earth
Armor of steel; and instant all the air
Was full of tumult and of cries and crash
Of swords wielded with might.
      Zobeir sprang up,
Lover no longer, but a soldier fierce.
With sword in hand, he dashed out of the tent,
Seeing but dimly in the dusky night
The shapes of men and steeds; yet knew a horde
Of desert Arabs, bandits jackal-like,
Had fallen on the sleeping caravan,
Greedy for plunder as a flame for food.

With such a mighty cry of burning rage
As a great lion wounded gives, Zobeir
Rushed on them, dealing blows as terrible
As Judgment Angels give with iron mace.
Like a wild whirlwind swept he through the camp,

While robbers fell before him as the corn
Goes down before the blast.
      At last he came
Unto the women's tent, wherein was placed
The fair Sakina, treasure beyond price
Intrusted to his hand.   Instead of song
And babbling laughter, through the curtains came
The sound of shrieks and wailing; while around
The battle fiercest raged, as when men fight
Around the sacred standard of a host.
The torches, lit in haste, with flickering glare
Lighted the combat, sending up their smoke
Vibrating like the tongues of dragons quick
To gather at the scent of blood.   Their glare
Showed to Zobeir how two stout ruffians came
Out of the tent dragging a woman veiled;
And as she shrieked, he knew again the voice
Which he had heard in song.   The word of death
From Allah's awful lips is not more swift
Than was his sword, doom-freighted, as it fell
Upon those ravishers.   As lightning-smit
They fell beside Sakina, dragging down
The cypress-slender maid into the dust.
But he sprang to her side and raised her; felt

Her hand, fear-cold, like a chill gem in his
Hot with the strife.   An instant through her veil
Her eyes glowed in the torchlight, meeting his;
And then again she was among her maids,
While he in mad delight, as one whose lips
Have drained a potent cup, raged madly on
In flame-fierce fury till the robbers fled.

When once again the morning found the world
The ground with blood was crimson as a rose,
And strewn with dead as is a threshing-floor
With scattered straws.   The broken caravan
Took its march silently, leaving behind
A place of graves amid the desert sands.

Still as they journeyed on, Zobeir rode close,
Guarding Sakina's litter, lest their way
Lead to some ambush.   All the day they went,
Halting not even in the burning noon
Lest the foe yet might follow them ; while still
Zobeir thrilled with the consciousness of her,
And of her nearness.   Drinking from a cup
Of mingled wine and gall, of woe and pain,
He rode beside her whom he might not see,
Loving her though he had not seen her face.

The waste was left behind, and when at eve
The caravan had halted, and the tents
Were pitched in a fair meadow where perfume
Of daffodil and hyacinth and rose
Made all the air sweet as the loved one's breath, —
When stars burst into bloom, while the old moon,
Worn to an amulet of silver, gleamed
With feeble light as if almost dissolved
In the dark sky; — once more Zobeir, enwrapt,
Stood by the women's tent, and heard the voice
Which was to him like song of Paradise
To one condemned never to enter there.
He stood foot-tangled in the snare of love,
And listened while Sakina trilled this song,
A plaintive lay which maidens of her land
Sing in the dusky glooms of cassia groves:

> " Sister fairest, why art thou sighing ?
> 'Dear one, a ring was on my hand;
> Now in the sea's cold deeps 't is lying,
> No diver brings it back to land.'
>
> " Sister sweetest, why art thou weeping ?
> 'Dear one, a rose bloomed on my tree;

  Some cruel hand while I was sleeping
   Hath reft my rose away from me.'

"Sister saddest, why art thou pining?
  'Dear one, I had a lover true;
Death smote him in my arms reclining,
  And I for death am pining too!'"

Zobeir felt his heart melt within his breast
As shadow melts in sunlight while she sang.
His strength seemed wasted like the dying moon
Which dimly watched him from on high. The cup
Of youth was emptied of the wine of hope;
The flame of joy was quenched; blackest despair
Compassed him like the darkness of the night.

Yet still his hand held fast to the fair pearl
Of honor with forlorn fidelity.
Through the night watches long he fought his pain,
And struggled with his passion as it were
Some fell beast which he grappled by the throat.

"O soul," he cried within himself, "learn thou
From the poor night-moth, which asks nothing more

Than that it be consumed in the dear flame
Of its desire. So be thy love, Zobeir!
No more my ears must hear her voice; no more
Drink in the raptures of her song; lest so
Love be too strong for duty, and I lose
All that is left to me in my despair, —
An honor spotless and a truth unswerved!"

III.

So wore away the night like melting snow,
Until the morning watch, when once again
The horde of bandits fell upon the camp,
Knowing its weakened force. Late, troubled sleep
Had spread its mantle on Zobeir. In dreams
He saw an image of Sakina, veiled,
Borne through the air in a vile afrit's arms.
A woman's piercing cry shattered his dream
As a blow breaks a crystal cup, and told
That once again the foe had found them.

                                                  "Lo!
I come, Sakina!" cried Zobeir.
                                        He leaped
Out of his tent into the whirl of strife
As leaps a swimmer into foaming waves
To save a loved one. Like the pestilence
He cut his dreadful way, and maddened wrote
His name on many a bosom with his sword,
Still struggling on to gain the women's tent.
But fate cast not that night the lot for him.

A slave behind him flung at him a stone
Which dashed him to the ground in headlong swoon;
And life's book seemed to close.
                                 When he awoke,
The morning glowed with saffron light, while he
Lay as the dead amid the dead. Like dreams
Which haunt the troubled night to flee with dawn,
Both friend and foe had vanished utterly.
No slave of all his train remained, nor steed,
Nor arms.
             "There is no god save Allah!" cried
With lifted eyes Zobeir. "What He hath willed
Will surely come to pass. But, O my love,
Not while I live will I forsake thy need,
If haply Allah to my hand will give
The joy of vengeance though He hath denied
The bliss of love. O thou delight of time,
Fate lead me to thy ravishers, and give
A sword into my hand keen as my rage,
Strong as my need! O heart-inspiring one,
How would I cherish thee if thou wert mine!
Should but a jasmine leaf offend thy foot,
I'd pluck up every jasmine of the plain!
Thy simple presence were unto my soul

As is the Tuba-tree of Paradise,
Whose boughs bear every blessing."

                                            So while pain
More cruel than from poisoned spear-wound burned
In his sad bosom, went Zobeir his way,
Following the track the robbers careless left
Secure that only death remained behind.
With no companion save his sighs he walked,
Plain leading on to plain, hill following dale,
While round him waxed the day in fervent heat
Which ripened the red grapes upon the vines.
Fainting and foodless through the weary hours,
With parching throat and aching eyes, and limbs
Trembling with pain, under the burning sun
Zobeir still followed steadfast on his quest;
Till the day waned at last, and like the kiss
Forgiveness gives remorse, the evening's cool
Descended on his throbbing brow. The stars
Unveiled themselves in heaven one by one;
The fine acacia leaves folded themselves
For sleep; the grass washed with its tears his feet;
And yet Zobeir pressed onward, till at last
He saw upon a hillside set with trees
A pitched tent and a kindled fire.

He crept,
Eager yet fearsome, through the sheltering trees,
Dragging his weary feet with cautious steps,
When suddenly upon the night air broke
The sound of singing, and his heart stood still
Because it was Sakina's voice which sang.
A melting sadness mingled in the lay
With piercing sweetness, as of hearts which break.
Only the white-winged angel Israfael,
Whose heart-strings are a lute, the sweetest voiced
Of Allah's creature's, might surpass that song.
Listening, Zobeir felt his tears dropping down
As pearls fall from a broken cord; while she,
Unseen yet loved, sang to a rebec thus:

"As a leaf that is tossed on the wind,
    As a lost tear the ocean waves drink,
  Are we blown on the whirlwinds of life,
    In the billows of fate do we sink.

"For the word that has flown from the lip,
    And the love from the heart doth outflow,
  Even Allah Himself may not bind,
    Wherever they hasten for woe!"

And hardly had the song died on the air
When two tall Arabs came from forth the tent,
And stood beside the thicket where Zobeir
Crouched full of ecstasy to hear those tones.

"Nay," cried out one in voice of rage; "no more
Thy words can stay me. We have left the tribe,
And have this charmer here alone."
         "Not so,"
The other answered; "since the tribe must be
Wherever we may be, and we are sent
To do its mission. It has trusted us
To bring this maid to Asim, he who now
Is but the Caliph's brother, yet shall be,
When the new moon is come, Caliph himself.
This gift shall win high favor for our tribe,
And show him how fate from his brother takes
To give into his hand, as it shall give
The kingdom and the sceptre. Let not now
Thy headstrong and unbridled passion bring
All our conspiracies to naught. So soon
We shall have sacked the Caliph's palace, shared
His slave girls and his wealth, that thou shalt have
Damsels enough without this singer. Now
Thy heart can bridle its fierce love, — and shall!"

"But where is damsel with a voice like this?"
He cried; "with bosoms like twin ostrich eggs;
With mole upon her temple like black pearl;
With blush like wine held to the light? Her eyes
Are whirlpools where despairing hearts are drawn
To swift destruction! While her voice in song
So sweet, so potent, so subduing is
That it could charm the angel Asrael
Till he forbore to smite though Allah bade!
What is this Asim then to me, that I
Should lose the fairest woman earth has known
To make him Caliph?"
     So with windy words,
Hot as a lion's breath, they quarrelled there,
While close behind them crouched Zobeir, and heard
Of Asim's treason till he knew the whole.
Long the two Arabs talked, one fierce to take
Sakina for his own, while cunningly
The other played upon him, dazzling him
With pledge of spoil and damsels should be his
When they had slain the Caliph; till at last
He cried, in acquiescence full of greed:

"Let it be so. To Asim we will bear
This night-dispelling maid, and haste again

To join our tribe ; for this old moon is worn
Almost to a thin thread, and with the new
Comes our reward.　I stay my thirst till then ;
But then I shall drink fountains dry !　Oh, then
Not one maid for my arms, but scores ! "
                                            " And so,"
The other said, " it shall be.　Now to sleep ;
Since we must ride under the morning star."

IV

The silence of the night fell round Zobeir;
The wasted moon above 'mid the white stars
Watched like the eye of fate what should be done.
His weak hand trembled, while upon his brow
The drops stood thick and cold.   Long crouched he
    there,
Then rose at last and crept toward the tent,
While thronging shadows followed him like djinns.

"Alas!   My strength is gone," he groaned in heart,
"Like the lost firmness of a withered reed!
My hand is empty; oh, had I but here
The meanest weapon!"
                      At the word his foot
Trod on a wood-knife by the dying fire.

Almost a cry of joy burst from his lips
As he laid hold upon the weapon.   Strength
Came back to him, and weakness seemed to fall
From off him as one drops a beggar's robe
Which hid his armor till in such disguise
He gained the hostile camp.   Stealthy as shame,

He slid like a thin shadow to the door,
Undid the curtain fastenings, and slipped through
Into the dim-lit tent.
      With eyes which shone
Above her veil as from the covert shine
The eyes of hurt gazelle, Sakina sat
Leaning against the tent-pole while she watched.
He laid his finger on his lip, and she,
As if she knew his face and welcomed him,
Pointed with slender finger, guiding him
Where it was safe to step.
      Through the dark tent
As steals a dream upon a sleeper, swift
Zobeir stole on one robber, and thrust through
His throat ere he could wake. The other sprang,
Awakened by the blow, and caught his sword,
Shouting the war-cry of the tribe, but fell
Cleft to the chin, the word yet half unsaid.

Then veiled Sakina leaped up joyously,
And ran unto Zobeir, and bowed herself
With mingled tears and laughter.
       "O my lord,"
She cried in tones sweet as from silver cup

Are struck by wand of ebony; "I said
Within my heart that hadst thou not been slain,
Thou wouldst have rescued me; and from the dead
Allah hath raised thee, and the word is true!"

"There is no god save Allah," said Zobeir;
"Surely it is His hand hath led me on
And given strength to strike; but now I faint.
I pray thee give me food and drink, — but lift
Not from thy love-compelling face thy veil.
It is not lawful I should look on her
Who is the Caliph's."   But within his heart
He dared not see her loveliness, lest so
The cord of self-restraint slip from his grasp.
Therefore she served him veiled, and gave him food
Stale wheaten cakes and dates as dry as dust,
With draughts of sour wine which kept the tang
Of goat-skin bottle, — yet to him it seemed
Like angels' food, brought by Sakina's hand.

And while he ate, she spoke of what befell
When he was left as dead and she was borne
Unto the bandits' camp. She told how all
Made ready for revolt, and openly

Boasted that Asim to their hands would give
The Caliph's palace for a spoil, with wealth
Of gold and slaves to pay their treason's price.

"These whom thy glorious hand hath slain," she said,
"Were sent to Asim that they learn his will;
And I was chosen from the spoil, a gift
Which should delight his eyes and win, perchance,
Favor and pardon if upon the day
When Asim falls on Bagdad with his hordes
As falls the locust plague on ripening grain,
The tribe should ravage other palaces
Not given to their hand by his consent.
As sure and greedy reach they for the spoil
As hungry boys reach out to pluck ripe figs!"

"Now, by the Prophet's beard!" cried out Zobeir,
"There is a serpent in that fig-tree hid,
Shall sting them in the plucking!"
       Thus they talked,
And when the night before the morning paled
As one might pale who saw death drawing near,
Zobeir saddled the tethered horses, steeds
Thin flanked, slim limbed, full breasted, barbs which
  moved

Beneath the rider like a bounding wave;
And they rode onward, over hill and dale,
The way to Bagdad. Ever as they rode
He fought with his hot heart, a strife more hard
Than had been combat with his fiercest foe.
And as they checked their steeds, once and again
Sakina's crystal voice, like lark escaped
From out its cage, broke forth in joyous song.
But with excuse that lurking foes might hear,
He hushed the sound which pierced his very soul.

And once behind her veil she sang this song,
As if her heart and voice communed alone:

   "The diver dared the swirling deeps,
      And brought the pearl to day;
   Then laid it in his monarch's hand,
      His tribute thus to pay.

   "Ah, diver, hadst thou kept the pearl
      Thou from the deeps did bring,
   Possessed of that, though now a slave,
      Thou then hadst been a king!"

"Peace!" cried Zobeir; "I must not hear thy voice.
Already it hath madness in me wrought
And kindled love!"
      While in his heart he said:

"Doth she not tempt me?"
        So he drew apart,
And spoke no more to her, but rested not
Till he had brought her to the Caliph safe.

V

So came Zobeir to Bagdad, and as one
Who lays his life down, to the Caliph gave
The damsel he had brought; and told him all
That had befallen. Flame-keen was the wrath
Which filled the Caliph when he heard.

          "Be quick!"
He cried. "Let twice ten companies go forth
And sweep the land as with a besom! Leave
Not one of all that bandit spawn alive!
Search every crevice in the hills, and dig
Into the bowels of the nether earth
Rather than one escape."

      Then to Zobeir,
Who waited in his presence, graciously
He turned the face of royal favor.

           "Thou,"
He said, "shalt wear the robe of honor. Speak;
Tell unto me thy very heart's desire."

"May my soul be a ransom for thy feet,
Commander of the Faithful," said Zobeir,

With downcast eyes. "Alas! within my breast
The restless wasp of unfulfilled desire
Still stings without surcease. Bid me go forth,
And wander through the world, till I may find
Some respite from this pain, some healing balm
May cure the smarting wound."

"Nay, by my beard,"
The Caliph answered; "dost thou think I hold
So lightly service such as thine? I lose
A host in losing thee. Tell me thy woe.
Haply I may bring comfort, for my hand
May even reach so high as the top bough
Upon life's tree, to pluck for thee that fruit
Which thou despairest of."

"No hand for me,"
Zobeir said, "plucks that fruit for which I die.
I love one whom I have not seen; I pine
For one whom I may never look upon.
Love bears me on like an unbridled steed,
Yet am I like to one who loves a dream.
I heard an unseen damsel sing, and fate
Hath wrought such madness in me that all peace
Is fled like arrow shot from a strong bow.
Honor's cold gem I snatched from love's hot flame

Since I was faithful to my trust; and yet
I am as a torn page in sorrow's book!"

"Yet tell me what divinest maid unseen
Hath kindled thus thine heart. The Caliph's arm
May reach afar; strong is the Caliph's hand.
Speak thou this rose-embodied zephyr's name."

Pale grew Zobeir as maid who lifts the cloth
From a dead face and sees her lover slain.

"Lord of my life," he cried, "not mine the fault!
Sakina's voice hath flown into my heart
As a bold swallow flies into a mosque.
I have not raised her veil, or sought to see
With love-delirious eyes her matchless face.
Allah hath sent this doom upon me; thou
Canst not be angry though I love thy slave,
For I have kept my faith, and thou shouldst pour
The oil of pity on my smarting wounds!"

The Caliph stood in silence, hearing all
With face which showed no more his secret thought
Than shows the palace wall what is within.

The moments fell like ashes from a brand;
While hotly beat the sad heart of Zobeir.

"But whither," asked the Caliph, "wouldst thou go?"

"All roads are one to him who seeks a grave,
He shall not miss his goal," Zobeir replied.
"But I will seek some trysting-place of swords.
I will drink war like wine; wed spear and shield.
When in the long array of battle stand
The warriors like the lashes of a maid,
And horn and cymbals shout, then man is man,
His own true, godlike self, and may forget
The petty passions that have snared his heart
In the poor days of peace! I may forget,
When war shrieks in mine ears, that witching voice
Which now rings through my soul. He whose lips thirst
To drink of valor's cup, forgets love's draught."

"Alas," the Caliph said, "how weak is man!
Doom bends him as the breeze sways rising smoke;
His best endeavor alters not his fate
More than the wind turns from its course the beam.

The palace of his hope, when destiny
Smites with its blast, proves frail as spider's house.
But I will be thine aid. What thou hast done
Is in the tablets of remembrance set;
Yet there is still a thing to do ere thou
Canst wear the robe of honor I shall give.
Go thou to Cufa. Take what band thou wilt;
Bring me the head of Asim."

"Nay," Zobeir
Made answer, "none shall share with me this quest.
What needs a soldier save his heart and sword?
If so be Allah to my hand will give
The traitor, it is well; — and it is well
If He hath meant this mission for my death."

So on the second day he rode alone,
Like one who flees, and can endure no more.
Bagdad was like a pool of burning flame
Since there Sakina was another's joy.
The world seemed space too small to put between
His heart and this great torture, though he knew
The heart bears its woe with it where it goes.

VI

Lonely to Cufa went Zobeir his way;
But when he came he found not Asim. Doubt
Had filled the traitor's heart when from the tribes
Came not the messengers, slain by Zobeir;
Since he who hatches treason fears unfaith
Even in those knit closest to his heart.
So Asim had set forth to seek the hills;
And thither turned Zobeir to follow him,
Caring not where he went or what befell
So only he brake not his loyalty.

And ever as he went he thought of her.
Her voice clung like a jewel to his ear;
Her presence compassed him about like light.
Where lonely palm-trees lift their tufted fans
Against the keen blue sky, he musing rode;
Or where the thick-set stars lit up his way
Along some mountain gorge, enwrapt he went,
In waking dreams of her. The long day through,
Weary of life apart from her, he sighed:

"O lingering day, why are thine hours so long!
Thy sun is like a tired runner, spent
Ere half his course is passed.   Oh, hasten on,
And bring the blessed night!"

         By night he cried:

"O lagging night, thou dost not onward move!
The Pleiads hang like clusters on a tree,
And drop not down the sky.   O day, come soon!"

It chanced one nightfall that he paused at dusk
To eat his evening meal beside a grove
Of great chinâr-trees; and as lone he sat,
His horse beside him cropping the short grass,
He strove to ease his sorrow with a song,
While hot tears to his eyelids pressed like doves
Which beat against their prison to be free.

 "Oh, let night speak of me, for day
  Knows not how breaks with woe my heart;
 Day knows not how I mournful stray,
  Weeping for thee, so dear thou art.

 "The sad night weeps with me, and lays
  Her tear-wet cheek against my own;

>   Although I walk in sun-lit ways,
>   Still doth my heart in darkness moan.
>
> "The night shall speak of me, and say
>   All things to thee I dare not show;
> And to thy dreams my love display,
>   Till thou art melted by my woe!"

And as he sang, from forth the covert crept
One in a garb had once been princely, now
Torn as by thorns and stained by way-faring.
Hunger and fear looked from the stranger's face
Like scared wolves from the thicket. Totteringly
He came and knelt before Zobeir, and bowed
His forehead in the dust, and trembling said:

"Surely we are twin bubbles borne upon
The bitter billows of the sea of woe;
Therefore thou shouldst be pitiful to me.
There is no god save Allah; by His ruth
I supplicate thy mercy, thou who art
A tree of hope in this world's garden. Lo,
I cast my life into thy hand; do thou
Preserve it as thine own, lest at the last
Allah should hold thee guilty of my blood!"

"Think not," Zobeir made answer, "that my grief
Thou canst divine from that poor song. Let be,
In Allah's name, to ask my secret pain.
It needs not that to make me pitiful.
Need is a plea for aid unanswerable."

Then to the fainting he gave food and drink,
And after asked him:
                "Whither dost thou come?
And what hath brought thee to these bitter straits?"

The other bent and whispered, as he feared
The tall chinâr-trees or the clustering shrubs
About their feet, might hear the word he spoke:

"I am the Caliph's brother; with the tribes
I plotted for his throne; but he hath swept
The tribes from off the earth. Some secret voice,
Some traitor base who hath betrayed our trust,
Hath told him what was done; and not one man
Is left of all my followers: while I
Have scarce escaped alive, and for three days
Have wandered foodless in the wilderness,
Till Allah sent thee to mine aid."

"And I,"
Zobeir spoke, "have been sent to bring thine head
Unto the Caliph."
　　　　　　　For a breathing space
Asim was silent, while his burning eyes
Were wild with horror and despair; but then
The passion of his fear broke forth.　He fell
To grovel in the dust, and kissed the hem
Of his pursuer's robe.
　　　　　　　"Now Allah judge,"
He cried, "betwixt us in the Day of Fear!
I trusted to thy mercy, and my lip
Tastes yet thy salt."
　　　　　　　"Nay," said Zobeir, "I gave
No food in covenant of friendship.　Alms,
In Allah's name, I gave the starving one.
Yet think not, Asim, that I seek thy life,
As thou hast sought thy brother's.　I will plead,
When we are come to him, that he forgive."

But Asim wept with scalding tears, in dust
Abasing his ignoble head, which once
Had been more proud than top of cypress tree;
Pleading for life with passion so inflamed

That half Zobeir was moved by pity, half
Stirred by contempt, until he swore to guard
The life of Asim as his own. Yet though
The traitor urged him sore that he might flee,
Zobeir consented not that he escape;
But brought him bound to Bagdad. There he fell
Before the Caliph's feet.

      "Lo, I am come,"
He said; "and bring thee Asim here, thy foe,
As once I brought Sakina, that fair maid
Worthy to wear green robes in Paradise."

"Thou hast done well," the Caliph made reply;
"Say now what recompense will please thee well.
Shall it be jewels or fair singing-girls,
Or gold or robes of honor?"

      But Zobeir
Unmoved made answer:
      "The one boon I crave
Is but thy brother's life; for I have sworn,
When he had, fainting in the wilderness,
No food save hunger and no drink but thirst,
To count his safety and mine own as one."

The Caliph's brow foreboded coming storm.

"Art thou, too, turned a traitor? Is the pearl
Of thy fidelity thus stained, that thou
Shouldst plead for him who would have slain thy
    lord?"

"Nay," he made answer; "I have proved my truth.
My lord, I am thy slave to do thy will;
To eat the bread of sorrow if thou wilt
And drink the waters of affliction. Yet
Above thy state is Allah, in whose name
I swore to save this man alive, or give
My useless life for his, since he has thrown
The arms of trust about my neck. My life
I offer thee for his. This world goes by,
And nothing in it is of worth enough
To buy man's honor, though his truth may burn
His heart as with a flame."
                        For such a time
As one unharmed might hold a lighted brand
They stood there face to face; then to the guard
The Caliph gave his brother, while he led
Zobeir into his closet.
                "List!" he said.

From some near inner chamber joyous came
The sound of song which flew like lark light-winged,
Fluttered and sank and rose and fell again,
Till all the air seemed sweet with fragrancies,
And quick with the remembrances of love.
It was Sakina's voice which sang within,
Piercing the sad heart of Zobeir with shaft
Of anguish tipped with keenest point of bliss.
She sang this song wherein a maiden tells
Her warrior-lover's might and gentleness:

> "When my love shouts in war,
>   Men think the trumpet blows;
> His henchmen thrill with awe,
>   While terror strikes his foes.
>   But when into my ear
>   He murmurs words of love,
>   My heart stands still to hear
>   That voice like cooing dove.

> "When my love wields his brand
>   None may oppose his might;
> None may his strength withstand,
>   And champions take to flight.

> But when his hand he lays
>   With softest touch on mine,
> I think a zephyr stays
>   To give me kisses fine!"

And as he listened ecstasy and pain
Struggled together in Zobeir's full heart
Like dove and falcon grappling in mid-air,
Falling and fighting as they fall.
                       "Tell me,"
The Caliph said, "dost thou not know that voice?"

"Nay," cried Zobeir, with proudly lifted head,
Though he was pale as withered cyclamen.
"Such a voice knew I once; but from the day
When she who sang was by my Caliph claimed,
I have forbid my soul to think of her,
Or to remember that she ever was!"

"When thou hadst gone," the Caliph made reply,
"To do my hest at Cufa, I beheld
The fair face of Sakina, and my heart
Was hers to tread upon if so she would;
My spirit cried for her as desert sand
Thirsts for the dew of night; or as the night

Yearns for the morning. But the torch of love
She lighted not for me. Day after day
In the fair garden of her lips the rose
Faded; the round pomegranates of her cheeks
Wasted to thinness; and I knew her heart
Pined for some other, for some lover far.
So when I questioned, at my feet she poured
The treasures of her hair, weeping like rain.
'Lord of my life,' she said, 'may my soul be
Thy ransom in the Day of Fear! Pardon,
And pity me; for he who saved my life
There in the desert, — he who followed far
And saved again from bondage in the hills,
Bears my heart with him wheresoe'er he goes,
Although he knows it not. I would lay down
My very life to see him smile; or bear
Tortures of living flame to bring him joy
For one brief moment! Pity me, my lord!'
With tears in mine own eyes I raised from earth
That weeping moon of love, lodestone of hearts,
Strangling my passion ere its birth-cry broke.
'Lo, his,' I said, 'shall be thy love. To him
Thou shalt be given as his guerdon, when
He comes again from Cufa.' And she waits,

Glowing with love and hope as with twin flames
A silver lamp.   Give me my brother's life,
And take instead — Sakina!"

                        Through his lip
Zobeir set his white teeth ; upon his brow
Stood drops as thick as rain ; while from his eyes
Such agony burned forth the Caliph turned,
And would not look on him.   Yet he stood firm,
And steadfast said :
                   "The robe of infamy
Clothe me if I abandon his distress.
Even for love man may not sell his truth!"

"Nay," said the Caliph, "bid thy fancy dwell
Upon the melting ripeness of her lip,
On the fine fragrance of her night of hair,
On the high hollow of her instep's arch,
On the entreating glances of her eye,
On her neck's slender column, on the swell
Of her round bosoms like a citron globed,
On her slim fingers, whose caressing touch
Were joy too dear for word, on her clear voice,
Whose spell already holds thee in its snare!"

Zobeir bowed low his head as if his heart
Could not endure to hear.

      "Spare me!" he groaned.
"Art thou the tempter Eblis, that thou thus
Wouldst have me break my faith for earthly joys?
Love is for life, but honor for all time!"

"Nay; honor passes; only love endures,"
The Caliph said. "Love is eternity!"

Again Sakina's voice uprose.
      "Listen!"
The Caliph said again.
      Yet once again
That voice beat at the bosom of Zobeir
Like storm-tossed dove, entreating entrance there;
Each note as sweet as hope yet sad as fate
Because love still delayed its longed for face.

> "I said to the wind of the south:
> 'O gentle south wind, blow!
> Bear kisses to his mouth,
> And greet him from me so!'
> The gentle south wind blew,
> With softly mournful sound;

O'er hill and vale it flew,—
　　But my love it never found.
O love, dear love, so long away,
While I am lone where dost thou stray?

"I said to the wind of the west:
　　'O sweet west wind, make haste,
　　And waken in his breast
　　　Longing my lips to taste.'
The west wind swiftly sped,
　　With sobbing, moaning sound;—
Ah, thou canst not be dead:
　　Then why art thou not found?
O love, dear love, so long away,
Come; for I die if thou delay!"

"It is for thee she sings!" into his ear
The Caliph breathed. "Have pity on her pain,
And yield to me this boon,— which I might take
But that I love thee well."　　　　Then in the dust
Zobeir cast himself down, crying with tears:

"Oh, torture me no more! Love rends my heart;
But Asim trusted me! I cannot break
My faith."

    The Caliph stooped and raised him up,
And kissed him on the cheek.
        "Falsehood from thee
Is far as mountain-top from the sea's floor,"
He said. "I give thee Asim's life."
           He smiled,
And looked with glowing glance upon Zobeir.

"Sorrow hath loved thee as groom loves a bride;
And hope that soared like a light lark on high
Lies like a warbler dead upon the plain;
But thou at least art true."
         Then once again
He kissed him on the cheek still wet with tears,
And softly to him said the one word:
           "Come!"

Zobeir followed him blindly, knowing not
Whither he went, till they were come in truth
To that rich chamber where Sakina sang.
There he at last beheld his love; a maid
Straight as the letter Alif; slight and lithe,
A heart-enticing one, with lips as red
As the pomegranate's pulp; with brows of jet

Lined on a forehead white as mountain snows;
With eyes in lustre like the Pleiades.

Zobeir stood mute with mingled love and woe;
While sweet Sakina gazed with startled glance.
Then as she rose as springs a fountain jet
Into the golden sunlight, in his own
The Caliph took her small hand, feather-soft,
And led her to Zobeir.
     "Behold," he said,
"Sakina's voice and her sweet self are thine!"

THE END.

www.ingramcontent.com/pod-product-compliance
Lightning Source LLC
Chambersburg PA
CBHW020901230426
43666CB00008B/1270